ALMANAC OF SEAPOWER
1990

The Almanac of Seapower Vol. 33 No. 1 January 1990

THE·ALMANAC·OF·SEAPOWER

24 / Coast Guard

64 / Maritime

Navy / 122

Marines / 217

SEAPOWER FACTS AND FIGURES

Calvin H. Cobb, Jr., *National President*
Dudley L. Carlson, *Executive Director*
Kenneth E. Cornell, *Director of Administration*

Staff for this book

Editor, Vincent C. Thomas, Jr.
Editorial Advisor, James D. Hessman
Assistant Editor, Mary I. Tuthill
Contributing Editor, Brooke Nihart
Editorial Assistants: Judith Armbrister, Susan Higman, Margaret M. Skekel, Dian S. Thomas
Director of Advertising, Wiley Loughran
Assistant Director of Advertising, Liana Satterthwaite
Art Director, John Kaljee
Typographer, Michael Sheehan

Authors of Essays

Trevor Armbrister
Charles W. Corddry
Andrew E. Gibson
Thomas B. Hayward and Ronald J. Hays
James C. Irwin
Isaac C. Kidd
Alex Larzelere
L. Edgar Prina
Richard Sharpe
Don Walsh

Copyright © 1990
Navy League of the United States
2300 Wilson Boulevard
Arlington, VA 22201-3308

ISBN-0-944433-05-7
ISSN-0736-3559

INNOVATION.
COOPERATION.
LETHALITY.

The security of the fleet depends on defensive weapons to counter low observable anti-ship missiles (ASMs). By 1997, it is estimated that over 100 countries will have 40,000 ASMs capable of being launched from single or multiple sectors using air, surface or subsurface platforms.

RAM (Rolling Airframe Missile) is a versatile, rapid and lethal response to the growing ASM threat. Cooperatively sponsored by the U.S. Navy and the Federal Republic of Germany, RAM is the only fire-and-forget weapon system in production specifically designed to counter ASMs. With a high performance airframe and dual mode passive RF/IR guidance, RAM is extremely effective against high speed threats utilizing the most advanced countermeasure techniques. RAM uses existing ship sensors, and its modular design allows easy installation.

RAM, an effective, affordable weapon system designed by General Dynamics Valley Systems Division, will allow the fleet to "fight silent" in the sophisticated battle of the future.

GENERAL DYNAMICS
A Strong Company For A Strong Country

"Sea power in the broad sense . . . . includes not only the military strength afloat that rules the sea or any part of it by force of arms, but also the peaceful commerce and shipping from which alone a military fleet naturally and healthfully springs, and on which it securely rests."

Alfred Thayer Mahan

The Almanac of Seapower is dedicated—with the sincerest respect and greatest affection—to the men and women of the U.S. sea services and their families.

PREFACE

In the year that has passed since the publication of the 1989 edition of the *Almanac of Seapower*, our world has been witness to more upheaval than during any comparable period since World War II. Surprisingly, most of it has been peaceful, although there were some horrifying political uses of force, most particularly the brutal crushing of a peaceful protest in Tiananmen Square last June. All in all, the turmoil in the communist bloc creates a mixed bag of hope, vulnerability, and most of all, uncertainty.

It has been fascinating to watch the rapid opening of the Iron Curtain. Experienced statesmen and scholars candidly admit that they never expected what was taking place, and that they don't know what will happen next. As old problems diminish in scope, difficult new questions arise. Will *perestroika* work for the Soviet Union? What impact will *perestroika* and *glasnost* have on the Soviet military machine in the short run? Would their successful implementation make the Soviet Union an even more formidable adversary in the long run, or rather a potential ally sharing common interests with us against other threats? Will the Warsaw Pact remain a formidable military power? What will or should NATO do next? Will democracy truly prevail in Eastern Europe? Will the Common Market effect closer relations with the emerging new European democracies? Will the two Germanys unite? What should the role of the United States be amidst the dramatic pursuits of freedom by hundreds of thousands of people? Elsewhere in the world, how will China react to all that is taking place in Europe? What Third World countries will develop into formidable economic and/or military powers? Will the Soviet Union abandon its espionage programs and its support of Western Hemisphere client states? Will the United States remain an economic superpower, or fall behind Western Europe, Japan, and perhaps other countries? What can we do to arrest any decline?

When the Berlin Wall was breached, Western leaders unanimously claimed, with considerable justification, that Western military and economic strengths, backed by steadfast resolve, have been the principal reasons why the Warsaw Pact countries were changing their political and economic policies. But there has been insufficient focus on the contribution of seapower to these changes. To be sure, nuclear power and NATO land and air forces have been strong deterrents to war. But the U.S./NATO ability to maintain the freedom of the seas during the almost half century since the end of World War II has contributed greatly to the growth of economies in the free countries of the world and the maintenance of the longest period of peace in European history. U.S. maritime superiority has been a superb and effective counterbalance to the superiority of Soviet land forces in Europe, and the key to keeping major sea lanes open throughout the world—*e.g.*, the Persian Gulf.

In 1890 Alfred Thayer Mahan published "The Influence of Sea Power Upon History" a book that ranks with the writings of Sun Tzu and Clausewitz as to its impact on military thinking and philosophy. Its basic theme is that nations with powerful navies and supporting overseas bases are victorious in war and prosperous in peacetime. Some of the essayists in this edition of the *Almanac* and other Americans of great stature also have stressed the importance of seapower in maintaining peace, and anticipate its increasingly influential role in tomorrow's changing world. We would be wise to heed them, as well as Mahan, particularly as the dismantling of our military establishment becomes an increasingly popular idea with the media and some politicians as the vehicle for reduction of the federal deficit.

We must keep in mind that the Third World is evolving into a formidable economic and military presence. Some nations that can't feed their hungry populations are buying or developing weapons with capability far exceeding that needed for conventional defense. Several Third World countries have either bought or are working to produce ballistic missile systems. Many more countries are developing or have achieved chemical weapon capabilities, and some have ambitions as to nuclear weapons. It probably won't be long before a Third World nation mates a chemical warhead to a ballistic missile, threatening a new dimension in terrorism. Moreover, over 20 Third World countries collectively possess more than 250 submarines, a fair number of which are modern, quiet, and competently operated.

Lest we forget, it took less than 21 years for a nation decimated militarily and politically in 1918 to create its capability to commence in 1939 a campaign of submarine warfare that almost brought Great Britain to her knees in the early days of World War II. It was allied seapower that in due course neutralized the German submarines and played the major role in winning the war in the Pacific. Similarly, after the communists' unexpected 1950 invasion of Korea, U.S. seapower was one of the major factors that eventually turned the tide against the Chinese and North Koreans.

In short, we see a world undergoing rapid change, with our country looking for quick answers to difficult problems, believing what it hears, and disregarding what it sees. We sense a growing, and perhaps premature, belief that the challenge to U.S. interests posed by Soviet military forces and other threats has diminished to the extent that our defense posture can be substantially reduced. While the magnitude of the federal deficit is a matter of grave concern, and while reductions in some programs and commitments may be acceptable, we must not forget the importance of our sealanes to our national survival. We must maintain the capability to ensure the free and unimpeded use of the sea by all nations, especially in light of our own dependence on imports for economic survival.

As you ponder the wisdom of our distinguished essayists and the wealth of information in this eighth edition of the Almanac, we hope that you find it more informative, more thought-provoking, and more useful to you than ever.

Calvin H. Cobb Jr.

CALVIN H. COBB JR, *National President*

Navy Likely to be Service of Choice In Lean-Budget Times

The harshest blow for the Navy in 1989 was its recognition finally that the 600-ship goal was history. However traumatic, acceptance of this reality meant that energies could now be focused on "maintaining a balanced, fully supported force rather than attempting to achieve one that is larger, but potentially hollow." The quotation is from the Secretary of Defense's (Frank C. Carlucci) annual report to Congress in January 1989, for fiscal year 1990. A hollow force that achieved some symbolic numerical goal would be the last thing the Navy needed.

With good luck, which is to say with fairly stable funding, the present level of 562 ships might be maintained into the early 1990s. Battle forces will be organized around 14 aircraft carriers, the long-sought 15th battle group having gone the way of the total fleet goal—into the budget grinder. Secretary of Defense Richard B. Cheney's decision to retire the carrier *Coral Sea* a year and a half early, and thus hold at 14 carrier battle groups, was the major structural change in planned U.S. conventional forces since the Reagan buildup started in 1981. (The change was in fact foreshadowed as early as September 1981, when the new administration faced its first budget crunch. It had to cancel plans to reactivate the carrier *Oriskany* and give up 29 other ships through retirements and cuts in building plans.)

By CHARLES W. CORDDRY

CHARLES W. CORDDRY, now the dean of defense correspondents, has covered defense and foreign affairs for 48 years, first for United Press and since 1967 for The Baltimore Sun. He also has been a panelist on public television's longest-running program, "Washington Week in Review", since it first aired in 1967. Among his many awards is the Gérald R. Ford Foundation Prize for Distinguished Reporting on National Defense—Lifetime Achievement.

The inevitable now has happened and has been acknowledged, and so the Navy enters the new decade with what Chief of Naval Operations Adm. Carlisle A.H. Trost calls a "fragile balance" between current force levels and overseas deployment requirements. The state of that balance will be crucial in this time of shifting world political tides and lessened tensions, when the Navy, almost surely if paradoxically, will take on more rather than fewer burdens.

Accordingly, the next debate for the Navy will focus on commitments—the nation's worldwide defense undertakings, including alliances and agreements with more than 40 countries, and forward military deployments to back them up. Will present capabilities, very greatly improved in the 1980s, be sustained? Or will they begin to decline and cause an overhauling of naval commitments to prevent a further skid?

The Navy, after all, met its commitments during the 1980s, while it was expanding by about 80 ships to reach its present level. It handled both standing commitments and contingencies, including Grenada, Libya, Lebanon, and the Persian Gulf, with fewer or, anyhow, no more ships. And it did it, apparently, without undue strain and stress that cause sailors to dream of civilian life as a happier alternative. By and large, it stuck by its promise to battle group crews—no more than half their time on overseas deployments, the other half in homeports. As 1989 ended, Vice Adm. Jeremy M. Boorda, the Chief of Naval Personnel, could claim the best re-enlistment rates in five years. There should be more recruiting trouble than there is, given reduced numbers in eligible age brackets and high civilian employment, he says, but the Navy met or bettered all its goals for high school graduates (90 percent against a national rate of 72 percent) and for scores achieved by recruits in qualification tests. And it met its manning goals.

Yet the Navy lately has been behaving as if it were under siege and facing awful agonies instead of, just maybe, a favored status. It is possible, of course, that new generations need reminding of John Paul Jones, freedom of the seas, and all that. And no military service, even the one that expanded most under the Reagan buildup, is willing to bank on lasting good fortune, or even reduced good fortune, especially when the congressional dice roll the way they do these days. The Navy in any event seems to be moving all ahead to justify, of all things, the need for a Navy—and for a fleet always at least as large as the one of the moment, preferably larger.

"One key fact," says Trost, "underlies any argument against cutting U.S. naval forces: The United States is a maritime nation whose dependence on the seas is the bedrock of U.S. political and economic security . . . The sea is what ties us, our allies and our friends together and makes our relationships viable." To meet future, shifting challenges, "a Navy unrestricted in its mobility and capability . . . is something we simply cannot do without."

From this unexceptionable position, the Navy is waging campaigns on several fronts:

—To begin with the obvious one, and, over the longer term, possibly the futile one, it is fighting against further force-level reductions. Apart from detente, grand strategy considerations, and the onsets of Defense Department systems analysts who don't see eye-to-eye with the admirals, the Navy faces problems of block obsolescence of destroyers and attack submarines and overhaul and refueling of carriers in the 1990s. It had planned to lay up the Charles F. Adams-class (DD-2) and Farragut-class (DDG-37) anti-air warfare destroyers gradually from 1990 to 1998; now it has been directed to retire them by 1994, 22 of them in the next two years. There is no way that the more powerful Arleigh Burke-class DDG-51s (33 planned but none yet in commission) can replace them unit-for-unit as fast as they go out. Besides the destroyer layup, the Navy decommissioned 16 Brooke- and Garcia-class FF-1040 frigates in 1989 and has been directed to transfer 24 Knox-class FF-1052 frigates to the Naval Reserve Force over four years, 1990-1993 (but still hopes it can get that number reduced to 10). Vice Adm. William D. Smith, deputy chief of naval operations for program planning, estimates that with reasonable projections of likely Navy budgets it will be possible to sustain a 560- to 565-ship force for "at least two to three years." Ships coming out of the pipeline from Reagan-administration orders give some breathing room, but the trend for ships under construction is down—103 on the way on 1 June 1989, 92 on 30 September 1989, and a predicted 75 on 30 September 1990. And it would be a considerable optimist, without memory of previous plans, who expected shipbuilding to rise from a current average of about 17 a year.

—A second campaign is being waged against naval-arms-control proposals floated out by Soviet President Mikhail S. Gorbachev and his adviser, Marshal Sergei F. Akhromeyev, but not under consideration in any current negotiating forum. Naval forces are specifically banned by the mandate governing negotiations in Vienna to reduce conventional forces in Europe. And, U.S. negotiators say, the Russians have not tried to introduce them, although Soviet Foreign Minister Eduard A. Sheverdnadze touched on them in his statement at the formal opening of the talks. Moscow has spoken, however, of calling a "special international conference" and thereafter a United Nations Security Council meeting "to discuss matters bearing on the restriction and reduction of naval activities." This seems a bit on the grandiose side and intended for public relations appeal wherever it might be thought that "activities of the navies in the Pacific" could be regulated or that the Indian Ocean should be turned into a "peace zone," presumably barren of warships however innocent the passage. The Navy, in any case, is taking no chances, fearing that naval arms reduction might get caught up, in Trost's phrase, "in a whirlwind of compromise." Taken one with another, the Soviet ideas would, by any analysis, work to the disadvantage of the United States and inhibit free use of the seas by maritime powers. A portion of Trost's analysis, in a speech in September 1989, is worth repeating here:

"The Soviet Union . . . sees the need to diminish the U.S. sphere of influence, and in turn undermine our economic strength. Critical to Soviet success is the need to reduce U.S. naval presence around the world: In the Pacific, where the consensus of nations, including China, agrees that the U.S. Navy is critical to regional stability; in the North Atlantic, where the U.S. Navy can keep the lifeline to Europe open in the event of war on the central front; in the Mediterranean, where the U.S. Navy bolsters NATO's southern flank, maintains a favorable balance of power, and deters aggressive action in the Middle East; and in the Indian Ocean and North Arabian Sea, where the U.S. Navy has been instrumental in keeping the oil supply flowing to the Western world for over 40 years. In essence, the Soviet Union wants to drive a wedge between the United States and our allies and trading partners."

—In a third campaign, closely related to the first two, the Navy portrays itself as playing an increasing role in an uncertain era of seeming new detente and disengagement. In this vision, there lies ahead a sort of creeping reincarnation of the late 1960s Nixon Doctrine, which called for reduced American overseas involvement on the ground and switched more responsibility to allies in collective defense. The United States would provide a "nuclear umbrella" and back its commitments with sea and air power. President Nixon had Asia in mind. But this time the application would extend to Europe as well, stemming from East-West arms reduction agreements, budget stringencies and, possibly, new divisions of military missions between America and its allies. If this is to be the case over time, it seems quite logical to Navy planners that the Navy would play an increasing role as a critical element for stability on the European flanks as well as the central region. And it would certainly have a vital role if there were ever

a re-mobilization and return of ground forces to Europe via the sea lanes. A similar case is made for the time when the United States reduces ground forces in South Korea. The Russians' arms-control proposals for curbing naval operations suggest that the same ideas have occurred to them. Apart from U.S. military retrenchment on the ground of major allies, the Navy, like the other services and not a few civilian leaders, has discovered potentials for all sorts of mischief, and worse, in the Third World—all further justifying the vision of an expanding role. Trost points to 250 submarines in the hands of 21 countries and says 13 countries have, or are on the way to having, chemical warfare capabilities. In the late 1980s, the Pentagon's Commission for a Long-term Integrated Strategy, estimated that by 2010 there could be 40 nuclear powers, a power being defined as a country with a dozen weapons and the means to deliver them. The ability to produce other modern weapons—missiles, aircraft, tanks, artillery—is spreading. Immediately at hand is the so-called drug war in which the military services are increasingly involved. For surveillance and interdiction, the Navy presumably could have made good use of some of the frigates being sent to the Naval Reserve, destroyers being decommissioned and, perhaps, some of the 73 P-3 anti-submarine warfare aircraft that are being retired in this year's cutbacks. As for future disengagement and concern over conflicts outside of Europe, much of the handwriting has been put on the wall by no less a powerhouse than Senator Sam Nunn, the Georgia Democrat who chairs the Senate Armed Services Committee. Nunn is quite firmly opposed to any cuts in U.S. or European forces on the continent while the conventional-arms-control negotiations are in progress (except for fewer than 15,000 U.S. troops being returned as a result of the INF treaty eliminating intermediate-range missiles). To forestall European reductions and undermining of negotiating positions, he engineered a provision in the fiscal 1990 defense authorization legislation that put a ceiling on the percentage of all NATO troops that can be made up of U.S. elements. If the allies cut, the United States will cut proportionately. The message is: "Don't cut." But once an agreement is reached on parity between North Atlantic Treaty Organization and Warsaw Pact forces, the story will change. Senator Nunn put it this way in a speech at the International Institute for Strategic Studies in London in September 1989:

"Once a conventional accord is achieved, the United States will face an overriding political and economic imperative that has been delayed a long time. We *must* reduce the cost of our forward deployments worldwide, including but not limited to, cuts in our troops and dependents stationed abroad. This is inevitable when you look at the United States budget, when you look at the fiscal situation we are in today. This will require changes in the respective roles within NATO of the United States and the allies that

A Leader in EW–Worldwide

For over two decades, working with the Navy and Grumman, AIL Systems Inc. has participated from inception through every evolutionary step in the design and development of the ALQ-99 tactical jamming system.

Today, this system, which is currently installed on the Navy EA-6B Prowler and the Air Force EF-111A Raven, continues to demonstrate its dependability and versatility by providing unparalleled protection for strike aircraft operating in hostile radar environments.

The Originator is still the Innovator.

For further information contact: AIL Systems Inc. Subsidiary of Eaton Corporation, Commack Road Deer Park, New York 11729

AIL
SYSTEMS INC.

go well beyond the reductions in manpower and equipment likely to occur in the first phase of conventional negotiations—even if they are successful. I believe the time has come to look seriously at the opportunity for what I would call specialization through builddown. Each allied country should play the instruments it plays best rather than try to conduct the entire symphony orchestra in each country.''

An obvious point for any Navy planner to seize on is that the United States plays the naval instrument very well.

Nunn also sees specialization as calling for reduced emphasis on deployment of heavy ground forces in Europe. Instead, there must be ''more emphasis on rapidly redeployable forces capable of dealing with major regional conflicts or crises outside Europe, many of which also affect in a very large way broad Western security interests as well as ours.'' In Europe, the United States would give priority to providing air power, if adequate shelters and facilities were built as long promised. And this country would ''continue to underwrite NATO's nuclear deterrence.'' That could increasingly involve the Navy's theater weapons, in view of the elimination of mid-range ground-launched missiles and the allergy in West Germany to modernization of shorter-range missiles.

—Finally, on the matter of Navy campaigning against cuts and naval arms control and for a relatively larger role in a builddown period: It would be wholly unfair, in a time of heavy and growing top level emphasis on unified operations, to say that the Navy is touting its historic role as the ''first line of defense.'' But looking out on the rapid and unpredictable course of events in the Soviet Union, Eastern Europe, the Persian Gulf, the Far East and, certainly, in parts of the Western Hemisphere, and then factoring in the Sam Nunn prescription for overseas retrenchment, the thought must have crossed admirals' minds that this situation spells Navy. Choose any of, or all, the buzzwords that military men love—flexibility, mobility, readiness—and the answer, in Navy minds, must come up Navy. From low-intensity conflict to strategic nuclear deterrence, American responses call for naval action, not solely, of course, especially in the strategic area, but nonetheless for naval action. For practical and political reasons, however, the scene in the Pentagon and at the Capital is not going to unfold as if the admirals had complete custody of the script. The Navy, as a retired four-star admiral noted, got a reputation for being ''grabby'' during the 1980s buildup and for macho interpretations of the maritime strategy which distorted it. The other services, with their considerable power bases, are not going to roll over in this new time of competition for fewer dollars and with it, most likely, new disputes over roles and missions.

Naval reductions and planning problems therefore coincide with a new era when radical changes in the security environment will be the main certainty. But, as some resilient Navy planners are beginning realisti-

cally to accept, there is not necessarily a collision between the reduced numerical goals and the prospective enhanced role of naval forces. As the FY 1990 defense budget report said in rejecting a larger but potentially hollow force, ''there is no mathematical formula for determining 'optimal' force structures.'' Certainly systems analysis cannot confidently measure the value of, or divine an absolute number for, naval forces to be employed for presence and diplomatic influence in various situations; that is a political-military judgment call. Many such calls will be made in a changing, multi-polar world. Contingencies always are coming up.

In the past, plans for sizing the Navy have been based on meeting global commitments far forward and being positioned for the opening phase of a war with the Soviet Union. The requirement always came up at 20 carrier battle groups, but 15 were settled on as adequate and possibly achievable. In the early 1980s, there were 13 and now the buildup is to stop at 14, which planners hope can be sustained through the 1990s. In global war terms, this means a somewhat higher risk. But, as the planners point out, nothing in current Soviet behavior indicates any desire for war, however much capabilities are being maintained. The Soviet economy is a shambles still, for all of Gorbachev's efforts to restructure it. The Soviet empire gives signs of disintegrating. War surely is not in Moscow's interest. Moreover, all indications from arms control negotiators are that a pact will be achieved that greatly reduces the possibility of surprise attack and sustained conflict in Europe. So it might be fair to ask whether the risk with 14 battle groups today is as great as it might have been with 15 in the past when the West confronted a bellicose Soviet Union, on the prowl wherever oppor-

■ *The guided-missile cruiser Belknap (CG-26), flagship of Commander, Sixth Fleet, is moored at Gaeta, Italy, her home port. She hosted President Bush off Malta in December when he met with President Gorbachev.*

tunity arose and ready to bump ships that infringed its self-proclaimed 12-mile limit.

In the new and different environment, the highlight of 1989 for the Navy was its exchange of port visits with the Soviet Navy. Naval bases—Norfolk, VA, and Sevastopol in the Crimea—were thrown open to visiting sailors, with tumultuous welcomes in both places. As amazed as his crews by the success of the four-day call at the closed city of Sevastopol, Vice Adm. Raymond P. Ilg, deputy commander of U.S. Naval Forces, Europe and the senior American officer present, left persuaded that such goodwill visits might in time curb the arms race and facilitate agreements. More such port calls are being planned.

Thinking of future peacetime and war-prevention positioning of the Navy, with unreduced but changing commitments, naval planners now speak of concentrating anew on the service's basic missions: control of the seas to look after national interests and hold alliances together as overseas deployment of land forces diminishes; projection of U.S. power abroad, and establishing a powerful presence whenever and wherever required. Maintenance and modernization of strategic deterrent forces is a given, though it may be said in passing that there will be future controversies over the mix of Navy and Air Force weapons for this purpose. Additionally, the planners look for increased exercises and exchanges of port visits with friendly navies and, of course, expanded anti-drug operations.

For some missions formerly regarded as highest priorities, it may become necessary to engage in random rather than continuous deployments if the strain on ship crews becomes too great. The thought of a less than fulltime presence makes Trost wince. Continuous presence is the optimum way to deter conflict and respond to crisis, he argues. But he would pro-

pose random deployments if decreased force levels or increased demands forced him to it.

"I do not favor a continuous presence short of a clear national emergency if it can only be achieved by exceeding perstempo [personnel tempo] standards," he told the writer. As an example of "random presence," he said a carrier battle group might leave an area, say, the Mediterranean, for a short time to exercise in the Norwegian Sea, and then return.

The point at this stage is to maintain the seapower the nation now has at the highest possible state of readiness within the resources that Congress is willing to make available. Senator John McCain, an Arizona Republican and member of the Senate Armed Services Committee, has put it this way: "Force-requirements exercises that call for higher resources will be only of academic interest, at best, and maritime strategies that smack of service parochialism will never be implemented."

One of the Navy's own, an aviator long in captivity in Vietnam, McCain put his service on sharp notice and read it something of a riot act in an article in *Sea Power* magazine in September 1989.

"We need to face the fact," he wrote, "that we must shift from a nuclear war posture and Europe-oriented strategy and resource allocation to a force posture and allocation of resources focused on the capability to project power anywhere in the world, and which assigns equal or greater power to dealing with crises in Asia, the Gulf, and the developing world. We cannot afford to waste money on forces whose priority is declining, while underfunding the forces we really need."

So far, so good. Then the senator went on, saying he did not necessarily mean shifting resources to seapower, and uncorked this:

"Maritime strategy does not mean buying a 600-ship Navy—a goal that was never justified by any supporting strategic plan, net assessment, or clear military rationale. In fact, if the Navy does not stop trying to justify total ship and aircraft numbers, and start showing how it can use its real-world resource levels to perform high-priority missions, it is certain to lose both its current force levels and its share of the defense budget."

McCain thought it would be a service if the Navy

and writers on sea power "never again mention the term '600-ship Navy.'" He wrapped up this way: "Our concern should be with finding the best force mix we can by implementing the strategy we need within the resources we can actually get."

And all this was from a congressional friend and veteran of the Navy. It surely underlines the point that it will not be easy to convince Congress and the public that there is critical underfunding in a defense budget of $305 billion—not in times when tension has subsided, the danger of World War III seems to be off the scope, domestic problems demand attention, and budget deficits seem to remain incurable.

Not underfunding but over-programming is the more likely complaint.

It is worthwhile to look back on a different time and see what lessons a builddown period can derive from a buildup hastefully put in motion.

In mid-May, 1981, barely four months into the Reagan-Weinberger "re-arming of America," Senator John C. Stennis sent up the first public warnings that the cost of the planned expansion would outrun even the enormous sums soon to flood into the military. Of the Navy's conviction that it needed precisely 600 ships to do its job, the Mississippi Democrat said it was unclear whether "such an ambitious" plan could be supported.

His worries reflected concerns already being heard widely, if privately, in many quarters, and they were to prove well founded. Ever the loyalist, the old gentleman—he was then 79 and had been a senator for 33 years—supported the buildup. But he admonished defense leaders in his long Senate speech that they had better be frugal, fix priorities, and get rid of waste, or they would lose public support. He cited already prevalent expectations of higher budget deficits, which surely would put downward pressure on defense spending.

The servicewide re-arming effort went forward with great vigor, as if all the deficiencies ever heard of would now be made good. By the testimony of officers now retired, money poured in faster than the services could decide what to do with it.

In the Navy's case, then-Secretary John Lehman soon was proclaiming that it already was too late to stop the 600-ship fleet; he had it on order. (He reckoned without future budget cuts and accelerated ship retirements.) Lehman had stated in early March a "major change in naval strategy"—publicized in due course as the maritime strategy—which lamentably seemed to overlook that naval strategy was an element of national strategy, not a thing apart from combined operations. The most arresting illustration of the new offensive thrust was Lehman's vision of carrier battle forces sailing up the Norwegian Sea to attack the Soviet Union's Kola Peninsula—where they arguably would face the largest single concentration of military power anywhere. Those were heady times for re-armers. Jeremiads were unwelcome, even from such a pro-military stalwart as John Stennis. If the

Soviet menace was going to subside, no suggestion of it had reached, or was thinkable to, the Pentagon of Defense Secretary Caspar W. Weinberger. He kept saying he hoped there was time to re-arm, but he didn't know how much time there was. What that meant was left to one's imagination.

By the middle of the decade, the Stennis prophecies became reality and another U.S. military buildup was on its way to a build down. Expansion plans were indeed too ambitious for budgets. Federal deficits soared. Waste and inefficiency abounded and priorities proved elusive. President Reagan had to appoint a commission (the Packard Commission) to try to get a handle on defense acquisition and overall management. (Cheney is vigorously trying to put its recommendations into effect in the course of implementing management reforms by which he expects to save $7.5 billion annually on acquisition costs by fiscal 1993.) In the Navy's case, the Congressional Budget Office concluded by September 1985 that the 600-ship plan would cost more than Congress likely was willing to pay. Instead of the "unprecedented" longtime real growth in peacetime budgets that the fleet would require, the CBO rather correctly foresaw a decade of average no-growth (other than inflation coverage) budgets. That could leave the Navy $250 billion short of its needs for the 600-ship goal. It had 534 ships at the time of the CBO study, a gain of about 55 from 1980. It had no intention of ceasing its march to 600. The adverse developments that Stennis and others anticipated at the start of the buildup led to many adjustments in what he called

■ *The flight-deck crew aboard America (CV-66) and all of her aircraft engage in both day and night flight operations.*

the "massive military program" (a program that, of course, brought massive force improvements). But it has yet to be brought within budgetary bounds. A prime lesson learned from the 1980s surely should have to do with matching plans and ambitions with resources—easier to do in times of plenty but just as essential, or more so, in times of austerity. Another

■ ADM. and Mrs. Arleigh Burke stand beside a plaque commemorating the keel construction of Arleigh Burke (DDG-51) during ceremonies at Bath Iron Works, Bath, ME, at the launching of the first ship of this guided-missile destroyer class 16 September 1989.

should be that Stennis was exactly right when he said it would be "nearly impossible" to hold public support for stepped-up spending unless there were demonstrated frugality and "decisive actions against waste and extravagance." The congressional signal about an end to defense budget growth is anything but indistinct. Administration signals on the other hand seem confused. Cheney recognizes, as he has said, that "real resources available for defense in the early 1990s are likely to decline." Yet until the recent dramatic development in Eastern Europe, Pentagon plans were being constructed on an assumption of real growth averaging 1.3 percent a year over three years. Requesting more than Congress is likely to provide is routine (except when there are agreements on totals, as in fiscal 1990). But the present course risks repetition of the early 1980s practice of putting more in train than can be afforded and then scrambling to readjust programs. Cheney cut enough, $10 billion, from the final Reagan defense budget proposal to meet the $305 billion target that President Bush and Congress agreed on for fiscal 1990. The major structural change, as said, was the deci-

sion against a 15th carrier battle group and the consequent layup of the *Coral Sea* a year and a half ahead of schedule. But certainly others are coming for all the services.

As the Defense Budget Project, a non-profit research and analysis organization, put it: The Cheney budget revisions "would not correct the long-term mismatch between defense resources and defense programs, and they fail to set forth a military strategy, or a sense of how military forces can adapt to a reduced level of funding over the long term."

Whether that is or is not too strong, the fact is that defense decisions for fiscal 1990 were driven largely by budget considerations, by the need to make inroads on the federal deficit. No strategic review had been completed when the decisions were taken. How else explain, for one example, greatly accelerating the retirement of Navy destroyers and surveillance aircraft that could contribute quite usefully to the anti-drug war? Or, for another example, the stretching out of F/A-18 fighter-attack aircraft when the Navy, as one admiral put it, is "kind of at the ragged edge" on aircraft?

For fiscal 1991, the budget deficit again will be a main driver in settling defense issues and those who believe Navy ship levels can be sustained concede that they may be working the optimistic side of the street. Beyond that, the peaceful turn of events overseas, U.S.-Soviet summits, assuming they go well, and arms-control advances are all likely to have a greater influence on defense posture—or desired defense posture—arguing in many minds for more reductions. It may be a deal harder to scare people with warnings about the Soviets as they recall the tumult and friendliness of Norfolk and Sevastopol, with the Soviet flag floating from American masts and vice versa.

To the Defense Department and especially the Navy, which sees the modernization of Soviet naval power going full ahead while older ships are tossed aside, Moscow's military posture still is adequately threatening to demand great caution. This does not gainsay that the Soviets' intentions have changed, that there is no sign they want war, and that they badly need peace while pursuing a numbing task of restructuring their economy. But it does say that all this change is still not irreversible and Soviet leaders have no intention of tearing down military capabilities to the point where their country is no longer a military superpower.

In summary then, the Navy is moving into a changing security environment in which it will take on more burdens while battling, maybe futilely, against further force level reductions. Whether smaller or larger than now, its capabilities across the spectrum of conflict and war-prevention suggest that it is likely to be the service of choice in a coming time of overseas retrenchment.

Building on success

1.

2. 36

3.

4.

5. WARR

6.

A decade of system innovation, development and deployment.

Perhaps the best way to judge the success of any naval program is by the phrase "at sea".

During the past 10 years, GE has completed development and provided currently deployed systems meeting critical operational requirements.

Building on this successful performance, there is more to come as we address the future to support continuing Navy challenges.

1. AN/SQQ-89(V)
ASW Combat System
Sensor, control and decision support systems integrated into a combat system enabling battle force combatants to conduct offensive coordinated ASW operations. *(Ingalls Shipbuilding photo)*

2. AN/SQR-19
Tactical Towed Array Sonar
Six times the performance of previous passive systems for detection, tracking and prosecution at tactical speeds.

3. AN/SQS-53C Battle Group Sonar
The world's most capable active sonar proven aboard USS Stump.

4. AN/BQN-25
Navigation Sonar System
Provides significant contribution to improved navigation of the Trident Submarines.

5. *Correlation Velocity Log*
Primary navigation sensor for gravity surveying aboard USGS research vessel.

6. AN/SQQ-30
Mine Classifying/Detecting Sonar
Principal sensor on the Navy's new Avenger-class mine counter-measures ship.

...and there is more to come.

GE Ocean Systems

Marines Face Challenge in Remaining Nation's Premier Force-in-Readiness

Deficits, debt, and detente are likely to mean smaller defense budgets and significant reductions in military manpower in the 1990s. While all the armed services are expected to take hits, the Marine Corps probably will suffer the least.

As the 1980s wound down, there were abundant signs that great changes were in the works. Severe economic and political problems in the Soviet Union were causing the Kremlin to ease its iron grip on its East European satellites, to tighten its spending belt, and to reduce its military forces unilaterally to make more funds available for the restructuring of the USSR's internal economy. These problems also prompted the Soviets to negotiate more urgently and realistically on the reduction of both nuclear and conventional arms.

As a result, there as been a diminution of the perceived threat to the United States and its Western partners in NATO from the USSR and its Warsaw Pact allies and a growing hope in this country that spending on defense can be reduced substantially in the coming years.

At the same time, the need in the United States, which is beset by huge annual deficits and a multi-trillion-dollar national debt, to bail out a portion of the savings and loan industry, to fight the war against the infiltration of drugs, and to provide increased outlays for social welfare programs, has put heavy additional pressure on the Pentagon budget.

With the risk of both nuclear and a conventional conflict between NATO and the Warsaw Pact seen to

By L. EDGAR PRINA

L. EDGAR PRINA served as a defense correspondent for the *Washington Star* and later the *Copley Press* for more than 30 years. For seven years he also was Washington Bureau Chief for the Copley News Service. He now is a free lance writer on military subjects.

be decreasing, there is a growing consensus that low- and mid-intensity hostilities are relatively more likely.

Gen. Alfred M. Gray, Commandant of the Marine Corps, rarely passes up an opportunity to focus attention on the need to be prepared for such lesser conflicts. Indeed, he has put great emphasis on this in Marine training and exercises. It makes sense, of course, for Gray to do so, because the Marines, with the Navy, would almost certainly be the first to be

committed to battle. That being the case, he argues, it follows that the Corps must be provided with adequate manpower and the best weapons that the nation can afford.

For the Marine Corps, the turmoil and change in the Soviet empire and the easing of what had been a confrontational attitude between Washington and Moscow, solidify its role as America's premier force-in-readiness.

White House and congressional support for a Fis-

cal Year 1990 defense budget, which cuts the Marines' force structure only slightly, indicates a broad acknowledgement of the contribution the Corps can make to national security.

In an interview carried in the November 1989 issue of *Sea Power* magazine, the commandant noted this and said:

"We would have to say that, on balance in these very difficult times, the FY 1990 budget that was submitted sends a pretty good signal about the impor-

tance of the Marine Corps.''

It also should send a signal to those ivory tower intellectuals and eye-shade accountants who recently stirred up the old non-starter idea of eliminating the Marine Corps by merging it with the Army. Their rationale: we now have two ''armies'' when one would do; accordingly, such a merger would make additional billions of dollars available for other uses, non-defense as well as defense. Abolish the Corps? It will never happen. It would be a political risk of the highest order for any president or member of Congress to advocate such a step.

But Gray has been criticized by some Marine officers who believe he spends too much time in the field with the troops and not enough time in ''the tank'' at meetings of the Joint Chiefs of Staff in the Pentagon, the better to defend Marine Corps interests. Some of the critics even feel that his virtual non-use of the term ''division'' could hurt if backers of the ''one-Army'' idea should attempt to overturn the statute calling for a minimum of three Marine divisions.

If these Marines are concerned about the ''one-Army'' idea, they don't like the prospect of ''two Marine Corps'' much better. As the battle for budget slices intensifies in a period of reduced appropriations, they fear the Army may make a bid for Marine Corps missions.

Although Marine Corps year-end strength was expected to remain at about 197,200 for FY 1990-91, there is no guarantee that its active-duty manpower will be spared in future budgets. Personnel cutbacks provide quick savings in outlays and have the added attraction of reducing retirement-pay costs later on. So Congress may very well continue to reduce America's active-duty rolls in the next few years, particularly if Washington and Moscow agree to major cuts in their conventional forces.

Gray already has said he would opt for a smaller Corps if faced with the prospect of significant cuts in procurement and operations/maintenance funds. The law says there shall be three Marine divisions and three Marine air wings, but it doesn't say they have to be fully manned or equipped.

The promise of force level stability for the next two years is not the only thing that the Marines are pleased about as the 1990s begin. Progress is being made by the Navy in its effort to reach the Joint Chiefs of Staff-approved goal in amphibious shipping: sufficient lift for the assault echelons of a Marine Expeditionary Force (MEF) and a Marine Expeditionary Brigade (MEB).

According to Gray, ''amphibious shipping requirements were protected very well'' in the FY 1990 budget. Funds were requested for one LSD-49, the cargo variant of the LSD-41 landing ship dock, and nine high-speed LCAC air cushion landing craft. For FY 1991, one LSD-49, one 40,000-ton LHD multi-purpose amphibious assault ship, and 12 LCACs have been requested. Congress, however, elected to autho-

rize procurement of 12 LCACs in FY 1990.

While 52 amphibious ships, including many LSTs (landing ships, tank) and older LSDs and LPDs (amphibious transports, dock) are scheduled to be decommissioned during the FY 1996 to FY 2009 period, the Navy's shipbuilding plans call for construction of 10 LHDs, 12 LSD-49s, and a new still-to-be-designed ship, called the LX, at a rate of three every two years until at least 15 are commissioned. The LX probably will be a modernized version of the versatile LPD.

But with every silver lining there is, it seems, a dark cloud. And for Gray and the Marines it was the proposed cancellation of their highest priority aviation program—the revolutionary V-22 Osprey tilt-rotor aircraft. Expected to be a key element of the Corps over-the-horizon (OTH) capability to land selectively and safely on enemy-held territory, along with the LCAC and the projected new armored personnel carrier called the Advanced Amphibious Assault Vehicle (AAAV), the Osprey was deleted by Defense Secretary Richard Cheney. The reason: its price tag ($27 million apiece ''flyaway'' and $28.5 billion program cost in FY 1988 dollars) and the need for spending constraints in the face of continuing large federal deficits and the $2.9 *trillion* national debt.

President Reagan asked for nearly $1.3 billion in FY 1990 and $1.6 billion in FY 1991 for 12 and 24 production copies, respectively, of the Bell-Boeing Osprey, a combination fixed-wing aircraft and helicopter. The amended budget agreed to by President Bush and Democratic congressional leaders led to the elimination of these requests. However, Congress did provide $255 million for continued research and development of the V-22.

Full-scale development MV-22s also are being procured on earlier appropriations and, as Lieut. Gen. Charles H. Pitman, deputy chief of staff for Marine Corps aviation, noted:

''We have not been asked to stop development. There has been no move by the Department of Defense or Congress to terminate development flight testing on which we have already spent $2 billion.''

This sparks a ray of hope in the Corps that some day, somehow, it will get an aircraft that can fly up to 300 knots with 24 combat-ready Marines aboard and then hover over a landing spot like a helicopter.

But what makes it particularly difficult to put the Osprey back on track is the fact that the Navy took what it feels was a disproportionate share of the amended defense budget cutbacks and that, within the Navy, aviation was hardest hit. Neither the Navy nor the Marine Corps feels it is in a position to give up other items of equal dollar value to keep the V-22.

It is Pitman's view that unless Congress, at the minimum, approves some advance procurement money for FY 1990, it will be ''almost impossible'' to start up the program again without significant commitment to tilt-rotor aircraft.

"We are pursuing other programs (at the behest of Congress) while hoping that somehow the V-22 survives," he said. "In the meantime, we are marching forward to come up with an alternative."

Ironically, Congress late last year voted to permit the Navy to spend up to $339 million—of funds appropriated in fiscal 1989—for advance procurement for the V-22, but the Pentagon declined the invitation. Deputy Defense Secretar Donald J. Atwood subsequently ordered the Navy to cancel production contracts for the plane. He said the move was "to protect the public fiscal interest" as the Defense Department did not intend to procure the aircraft.

Still, the Atwood order may not end the matter. The Osprey has strong supporters in Congress and, depending upon such factors as arms control talks with the Soviets and U.S. commercial aviation needs, the program may yet be saved.

Under the original plan that was cancelled, the Marines were to have procured 605 Ospreys and the Navy 50. Earlier, the Army had planned to buy 331 and the Air Force 55, but the Army dropped out of the program. For the Marines, the MV-22 would replace its aging fleet of CH-46 helicopters, while the Navy would use its Ospreys for search and rescue and other jobs.

The Marines studied alternatives to the Osprey, but did not find any that would provide the capability of the V-22, even at higher costs. Perhaps in the new study they will fund a cheaper alternative that would give them the lift they require, but with less capability.

It is clear, however, that any non-tilt-rotor alternative would not provide the speed and range of the Osprey. And that would be a blow to Marine plans for a faster, safer, stealthier assault force.

Marine leaders have been insisting over the last several years that the Corps has the best equipped and trained personnel in its history. But they have also said a critically important piece of capability at the tactical mobility level needed updating. That's where the V-22 was supposed to provide the answer with its ability to come to the target area from well over the horizon.

Coming from "well over" the horizon is essential for the success of any future amphibious and expeditionary operations from the sea, particularly in view of the proliferation of guided missiles, even among Third World countries. One only has to recall the negative impact shoulder-fired Stinger missiles had on Soviet air operations in Afghanistan to appreciate the point.

"Today, we can come from *near* over the horizon, but the amphibious triad of the V-22, the LCAC, and the AAAV would give us the capability to come from the sea in a total vertical mode as well as in the LCAC and the high-speed amphibian," Gray told *Sea Power* magazine.

"It opens up a whole new horizon in terms of where we can land, how we can shape the battle early on, how we can go where they (the enemy) aren't. It would give us enormous flexibility in terms of defeating potential enemy centers of gravity. So, the V-22 is a vital part of our concept."

The 50-knot LCAC, which can carry heavy artillery, 67-ton M-1 Abrams tanks and large-sized equipment, could be launched from 40 to 50 miles over the horizon. So, too, could the 75-mile-radius helicopters now in the force, but they would have little flying time to go around enemy deployments.

As Lieut. Gen. Carl F. Mundy, Jr., deputy chief of staff for plans, policies, and operations, put it:

"If you fly over (the enemy) you get shot down. The V-22 (which has an 1,100-mile radius) absolutely can fly around and angle back in to 100 to 150 miles beyond the main enemy defense."

In Mundy's opinion, the Corps itself is partly to blame for cancellation of the Osprey. "We have never really explained amphibious operations adequately to the public in general or to defense decision-makers and that, in part, was the reason for the decision on the V-22," he asserted.

He said too many individuals still think of amphibious operations in terms of the bloody frontal assaults at Tarawa and Iwo Jima in World War II.

Gray believes that the enhanced survivability provided by a V-22-type aircraft is perhaps its greatest asset.

"Our studies indicate that in combat the V-22 would be three times more survivable against a missile threat, and 13 times more survivable against a gun threat, than the alternative force mix," the commandant said. "The survivability features of the V-22 are designed to protect those most precious and irreplaceable of national assets—young men who have chosen to go 'in harm's way' in the service of their country."

As to cost, the Defense Department and the Corps do not see eye-to-eye. The amended FY 1990-91 budget request of last April contained a mix of CH-53E Super Stallion heavy lift and UH-60 Army Blackhawk utility-transport helicopters in lieu of the Osprey. Pentagon analysts believe this mix would be less expensive. The Marines challenge this conclusion, asserting that it would take a force of 950 Super Stallions and Blackhawks to do the work of 605 Ospreys while suffering more losses in the event of combat. The Marines also assert that it would clearly be more expensive to operate and maintain a force of 950 helicopters than a MV-22 fleet. They add that, given the trend toward lower defense budgets, the likelihood that the Pentagon would approve the purchase of that many choppers is remote.

Attainment of the Advanced Amphibious Assault Vehicle (AAAV), the third leg of the Marines' power projection triad, probably won't be realized until the late 1990s or early in the 21st century, largely due to fiscal constraints.

The Marines are seeking a vehicle that can move

The new *Yavuz* and the SQS-56 sonar make a

She's the brand-new flagship of the Turkish navy, and Blohm+Voss built her using their Modular Functional Unit System.

This new construction method meant that the Raytheon-developed and -produced AN/SQS-56 sonar, vital to this *Meko 200* class frigate's antisubmarine mission, was delivered housed in a single, completely integrated module. Once lowered into place through a deck opening, all the system needed was to be bolted down and to have its electrical connections hooked up. The Functional Unit System enabled the shipyard to install thirty completely functional weapons and electronics

systems in only fifteen days.

The *Yavuz*'s SQS-56 will enable her to locate and classify targets in either the passive or active mode. The system is compact and easy to operate, and has low life-cycle costs. Yet its detection ranges have consistently been the maximum possible under existing environmental conditions. More than 100 of these sonars are already being used by U.S. and foreign naval ships ranging from 720 to 3,600 tons.

Today, Raytheon has more sonars aboard naval combatants around the world than any other manufacturer. That leadership is the result of an intense study of the fundamentals of

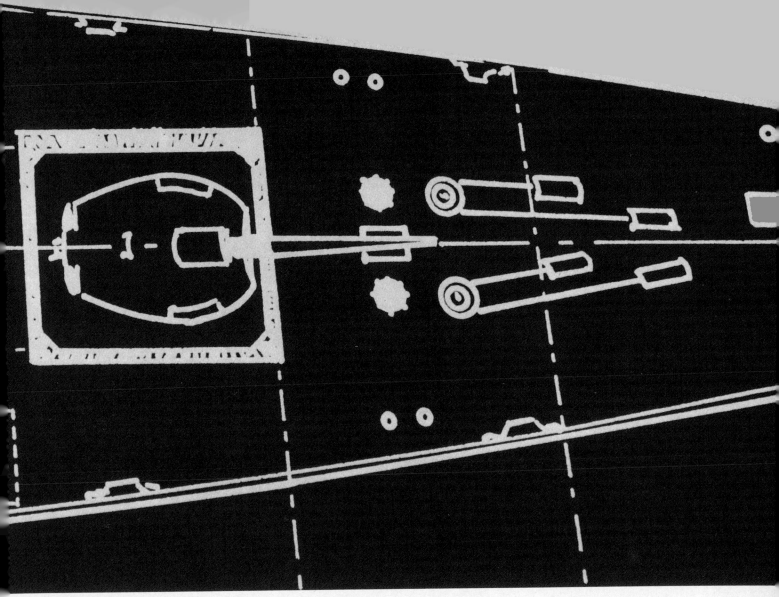

perfect fit.

underwater acoustics that began in
1901 and continues to this day.

For further information, write:
Raytheon Company, Government
Marketing, 141 Spring Street,
Lexington, Massachusetts 02173.

AN/SQS-56 sonar significantly increases the
***Yavuz*'s ASW capabilities.**

Raytheon

Where quality starts with fundamentals

over the water at 25 knots to replace the current 8 to 10 knot light armored vehicle (LAV-7), which was introduced in 1970. This likely will mean a type of hydrofoil or surface-effect craft, a vehicle that can get up on top of the water and "fly." Gray sees great potential in a hybrid hull which, unlike a pure hydrofoil, does not fully rise above the surface of the sea.

A test model of a Marine AAAV attained a speed of 29 knots at Patuxent River, Md., last year, leading some Marine leaders to exult over what they see as a major breakthrough in combat vehicle technology.

"We know now that we could build the best armored personnel carrier in the world that can do things in the water that must be seen to be believed—and at a price that will not break the bank," one high-ranking officer asserted.

Still, among other things, the Marines do not yet know the effect of this vehicle on the riflemen, who may have to ride it for 40 or 50 miles in a rough sea.

While Marines now only dream of what their power-projection capabilities could be if allowed to exploit technology available today, Gray's restructuring of the Corps to increase its readiness for handling low- and mid-intensity conflicts is all but complete. Now it's a question of implementation and fine-tuning the changes already ordered.

In 1988, the Commandant created the Marine Corps Research, Development, and Acquisition Center and the Marine Corps Combat Development Command at the Quantico, VA, base some 40 miles south of Washington. These organizations now are functioning as planned. He also continued the streamlining of Headquarters, Marine Corps (HQMC) in Washington and turned over reserve affairs to a three-star deputy chief of staff for manpower, who also handles active duty personnel.

Last year, the cadreing of three infantry battalions, made necessary when Congress cut Marine manpower by 2,900 in FY 1988, was completed, leaving the Corps with 24 battalions. Meanwhile, the action, called "painful" by Lieut. Gen. John T. Hudson, who retired late in 1989 as deputy chief of staff for manpower and reserve affairs, to tranfer nearly 3,000 Marines from the support establishment to beef up the Fleet Marine Forces (FMFs), is still under way.

■ *Marines engage in route reconnaissance during an exercise in Panama in October 1989.*

The new FMF structure includes surveillance, reconnaissance, and intelligence (SRI) groups in each headquarters and a fourth rifle company in reconnaissance battalions and in the eight infantry battalions involved with Marine Expeditionary Units (MEUs).

As for training, a few days have been added to the recruits' calendar and the content modified to incorporate basic warrior training. The two schools of infantry (Camp Pendleton, CA, and Camp Lejeune, NC) of advanced training for all enlisted male Marines opened for business last June. It is the first time all will get this level of training.

Hudson noted that enlisted aviation personnel, including staff sergeants, had no field skills or any idea how to organize a defense. He said the sergeants knew how to conduct parades and inspections, and they'll now know how to get up a defense.

For a number of years, first-term Marines were being re-enlisted in their military occupation specialties (MOSs) even if the particular category were overloaded with personnel. This caused big trouble and HQMC started last year to turn things around.

"Seventy-five percent of our MOSs were out of balance and critically so," Hudson said. "There was promotion stagnation and some MOSs were under strength. It was the worst thing we were doing. Now they are being re-enlisted in MOSs where they are needed."

Recruiting is becoming more difficult as the pool of young men and women continues to shrink, although Gray's goals for accessions of high school graduates (90 percent) and mental categories I, II, and IIIa (63 percent) were exceeded by comfortable margins. High school graduates are preferred to non-graduates, but not every one with a diploma meets even the average standard. "We get high school graduates who can't read at all and many with eight and ninth grade reading ability," Hudson said.

Retention in 1989 was at the historical average, but the year ended with a shortage of approximately 400 company-grade aviators. As a result, the Corps was given permission by Congress to pay bonuses to pilots just as the Navy and Air Force do. Although Marine aviators fly the same aircraft off the same decks as Navy pilots, they have been paid some $12,000 per year less, according to Hudson. Previously, the Marines were not authorized to pay aviation bonuses be-

■ *The controversial tilt rotor aircraft, the Osprey, which the Marine Corps long has sought to enhance its heavy-lift capability. Congress included $255 million in the FY 1990 budget for further research and development, but no more funds for its production were provided.*

cause they had no significant shortages.

In the opinion of many Americans, a young man doesn't have to be very smart to be a rifleman. Hudson couldn't disagree more. "It's absolutely a myth that you can take any dumb guy and he's a good infantryman," he said. "You can take any dumb guy and he can go out and get killed and get two or three killed with him. It takes brains and skills to be a good infantryman."

Gray, who enlisted in the Corps after high school and rose to become the 29th commandant, has taken a strong interest in military education for his Marines—officers and enlisted alike. He has overhauled the entire educational process in the Corps. Here is what he did last year:

• Started a professional military education program in which all officers and non-commissioned officers must participate.

• Upgraded the Command Staff College faculty with prominent civilian professors added to the staff and ordered curriculum changes to increase the focus on the interrelationship of the strategic, operational, and tactical levels of war within a joint and combined environment.

• Created a Marine Corps professional reading program for officers and non-coms featuring a systematic and progressive list of books and periodicals with relevance to warfare.

• Established the new Marine Corps University on 1 August. It includes four schools: Command and Staff College for majors, amphibious warfare for captains, basic for lieutenants, and the Staff Non-Commissioned Officers Academy for non-coms.

The new university also has a strong, fully comparable nonresident program.

Marine aviation may not get its tilt-rotor Osprey this year, but it has a number of things to cheer about, in addition to the bonuses for pilots. This summer, for example, it will take delivery of its first AV-8B Harrier vertical/short takeoff and landing (V/STOL) attack/close support jet with a new and more powerful Rolls Royce engine. The engine, which helped set four time-to-climb records in tests in England last year, has 3,000 pounds more thrust than the current Harrier engines and can go twice as long before an overhaul is required.

Deliveries of the night-attack-capable AV-8B and F/A-18D two-seater Hornet, which is seen as a replacement for the aging A-6 Intruder, began toward the end of last year and now are accelerating. The first squadron of these Hornets is due to become operational at El Toro Marine Corps Air Base in California in March.

Meanwhile, Marine aviation is "lightening up" its equipment to make the air combat element (ACE) of a Marine Air Ground Task Force more expeditionary. Some Hawk and Stinger air defense units have been transferred to the Marine Corps Reserve. Fewer expeditionary air fields, with their steel matting, are needed as more Harriers are delivered. And, eventually, no matting at all will be needed if testing of new mobile arresting gear at Lakehurst (NJ) Air Development Test Center is successful—as expected. The arresting gear package comes in on wheels and can be set up within an hour on any highway in the world, according to Pitman. It can handle a fully loaded F/A-18.

While simulators for aviation firing exercises are so good today that they do everything but provide the bang and the smoke, ammunition shortages have caused some reductions in training.

"We are getting to the point where the shortages of weapons are starting to impact slightly on readiness so that we can notice it," Pitman said.

The Corps began to draw down on its war reserve of ammunition last summer, just as it did in the late 1970s, but, so far, not nearly as heavily. Some munition stocks, prior to 1981, were down to a five days' supply, with the average running at 30 days. Currently, most Marine ammo supplies range from 46 to 60 days' worth.

A cloud somewhat bigger than a man's hand is hanging over the Marine Corps' operations and maintenance (O&M) budget. It was cut by more than 9 percent for FY 1990 and faces a similar reduction in FY 1991.

Marine leaders feel that the Corps can absorb moderate cuts without too severe an adverse effect by adopting such cost-saving measures as scheduling fewer large-scale and more small unit exercises and by doing more training closer to home bases. But they are concerned about the trend.

"If we continue to take the degradation in O&M funds that we have experienced in the last several years, clearly we may have to make drastic changes in the Marine Corps in terms of its size, force structure, and ultimately, in its ability to be as responsive as the nation wants us to be," Gray said.

In the area of equipment, the Corps benefitted from an unprecedented period of modernization in the 1980s. Gen. P.X. Kelley, the Commandant from 1983 to 1987, called the period "the golden years." Much of the Marine inventories of weapons, vehicles, aircraft, rolling stock, and supplies is comparatively new today, and the pipeline is still fairly full.

Lieut. Gen. William G. Carson, Jr., deputy chief of staff for installations and logistics, asserts that the Corps is in "better shape" in his area of responsibility than "I ever can remember in my 36 years in the logistics business."

To buttress this assessment, he noted that the Fleet Marine Forces and Marine reserve equipment readiness stood at 92 percent and 89 percent, respectively, in FY 1989.

Steady progress with the storing of Marine equipment and supplies both aboard the maritime prepositioning ship (MPS) flotillas in the Atlantic, Pacific, and Indian Oceans and ashore in Norway was also cited.

The Corps was to have completed its program in Norway in January 1990 for the storing of selected equipment and 30 days' supplies and ammunition for an air-ground task force of 13,000 men (brigade-size) to support its mission to help defend the northern flank of NATO. There is a shortfall in pre-positioned ammunition, but this will not preclude the Marines from meeting the initial operational capability date. They could, if necessary, draw ammunition from resources allocated to other commitments, according to the General Accounting Office, which reported to Congress on the Norway program last year.

Rolling stock, 155-mm towed howitzers, packaged petroleum, oil and lubricants, medical supplies and equipment, and rations are among the items being stored in caves tunneled into granite mountains to support the ground combat element. The caves are fitted with blast-proof doors. Aviation ground-support equipment, including cranes, aircraft tow trucks, and weapons loaders, are being pre-positioned at two air bases in central Norway.

Meanwhile, the second biannual maintenance cycle for the 13 fully loaded ships of the three MPS flotillas is under way; the first was completed last year. During the current cycle, Gray has directed the logistics experts to experiment with the loading of these ships to support a Marine Expeditionary Unit rather than a Marine Expeditionary Brigade, which each flotilla was designed for. The goal: to provide a faster closure time for the combat units.

As the maintenance recycling goes forward, modification work is performed, equipment exchanged and/or repackaged, some shelf items purged or upgraded, and bad lots replaced. It takes two years to complete the job.

Gray is well past the half-way mark in his four-year tour as Commandant. He has wrought major changes over the last 30 months, and now the Corps is ready to take off on a sustained run.

But his challenge from now until he turns over the baton to his successor in July 1991 will be to tighten the Corps' belt during an expected period of declining budgets and develop innovative ways to maintain the gains of the 1980s in combat readiness and sustainability.

The next Commandant, the 30th, is likely to face the same challenge. Will he make major changes of his own or will he accept the Gray restructuring in toto, most of it or only part of it? We can only wait and see.

New and Broadened Roles Make It Difficult To Maintain Traditional Flexibility

On the night of 23 March 1989, the 213,000-ton tankship Exxon Valdez *pulled away from the Alyeska marine terminal at Valdez, AK, and headed down Valdez Arm towards Prince William Sound. The 987-foot tanker was loaded with more than 53 million gallons of heavy North Slope crude; the ship was drawing 56 feet.*

Captain Joseph Hazelwood called the Coast Guard's Valdez Vessel Traffic Service at 11:25 P.M. and reported that the pilot had departed the ship. He informed VTS Valdez that the tanker would probably leave the outbound traffic lane, cross through the separation zone, and proceed down the inbound lane to avoid ice drifting south from Columbia Glacier.

At four minutes past midnight on Good Friday, 24 March, the two-year-old tanker, making 12 knots, slammed into Bligh Reef. The reef, 30 feet below the surface, ripped open eight of Exxon Valdez's *11 cargo tanks as the ship careened up onto the rocky ledge. Within five hours, 10.1 million gallons of thick black oil gushed from the ship's ruptured tanks, creating the worst pollution incident in the history of the United States.*

Three months later, while the clean-up in Alaska was in full swing, three more tanker groundings caused major spills on 23 and 24 June: 420,000 gallons of heating oil in Narragansett Bay, 250,000 gallons of heavy crude in Galveston Bay, and 310,000 gallons of industrial heavy oil in the Delaware River.

The series of spills made pollution the "high visibility" issue for the Coast Guard in 1989. When asked

By ALEX LARZELERE

CAPTAIN ALEX LARZELERE's operational career included duty aboard seven ships, five of which he commanded. He is a graduate of the Naval War College and the National War College, and recently completed a two-year research project as a Senior Fellow at the National Defense University. His staff assignments were in operations, personnel, and congressional affairs. He was the Coast Guard's first Aide to the President.

if he thought the pollution incidents would mean a shift in Coast Guard emphasis to environmental protection programs, Rear Adm. Joel D. Sipes, chief of the Coast Guard's Office of Marine Safety, Security, and Environmental Protection, replied, "Absolutely. We were headed that direction anyway. We were moving into preventative programs. . . . The administration was elected on an environmental ticket. Now, there's renewed emphasis."

Congress reacted quickly to the Alaska spill with members concentrating on environmental issues; they recognized the potential for devastating pollution incidents in other coastal areas. A plethora of proposed legislation dealing with environmental protection resulted. Virtually all of the more than 40 bills submitted require some action by the Coast Guard. In cooperation with Congress, the Coast Guard's legal staff bundled the various pieces of legislation into a single comprehensive proposal. The Omnibus Oil Spill Prevention, Response, Compensations and Liability Act was submitted for consideration by Congress.

The bill includes a full range of measures from prevention to compensation. One of Congress' first concerns was to develop systems to reduce the danger of future groundings and collisions; interest in Vessel Traffic Services (VTS) systems was revived. Four major VTS systems (Houston-Galveston, San Francisco, Puget Sound, Prince William Sound) and three minor systems (Berwick Bay, LA, Louisville, KY, and Sault Ste. Marie, MI) currently are operated by the Coast Guard. The systems, which have been allowed to languish for lack of funding over the past few years, are getting renewed attention. Congress quickly included $5.6 million in the Coast Guard's FY 1989 supplemental appropriation to reopen the New York Harbor VTS system, which had been discontinued.

Legislation directs the Coast Guard to conduct a comprehensive study of port requirements throughout the entire United States. Specifically the study will address the adequacy of existing VTS installations and the need for additional systems. A nine-member special projects staff began by reviewing the Coast Guard's 1973 Port Needs Study and Canada's 1984 and 1986 Port Studies. The new study, based on *risk analysis* as opposed to *accident analysis*, is considering geographical, environmental, and weather features of the nation's port system as well as analyzing shipping data and accident histories. The Secretary of Transportation, Samuel Skinner, will use the results to recommend system installations and upgrades to Congress. The objective: "The development of VTS systems which reduce the risk of marine accidents to the lowest level economically justified."

Secretary Skinner also will initiate rulemaking concerning vessel participation in VTS systems (classes of ships to participate and level of control over movements of vessels). If the final decision calls for mandatory participation in *control* versus *advisory* systems, a strong reaction is certain to come from the marine industry and pilot's associations.

Another study group, formed in the wake of the *Exxon Valdez* grounding, is examining laws and regulations governing pilots. Remarkably, the last change to United States pilotage laws was made in 1871—a time when ships the size and complexity of *Exxon Valdez* were beyond the wildest dream. The Pilotage Requirements Study is looking at a spectrum of vessel-control issues, including the extent of pilotage waters; requirements for pilots based on qualification of licensed shipboard personnel, nature of voyage and type of cargo; type and size of vessel; navigation equipment and pilot responsibilities. The group also will review the issue of jurisdiction—federal versus state pilots. Currently, individual states establish pilotage regulations for international voyages arriving from foreign countries while federal rules govern pilotage for ships sailing from one U.S. port to another.

As unfortunate as the *Exxon Valdez* grounding was, it created opportunities for the Coast Guard to review and improve existing laws and regulations. "Eighty percent of all ship accidents are the result of human error," Sipes said. "The Valdez accident presents an opportunity for us [Coast Guard] to take a hard look at personnel issues. The standards of training, certification, and watch standing need to be looked at." Sipes said the issue of double bottoms (watertight subdivisions separating tanks from the skin of the ship) is a long-standing and controversial one that will be reopened as a result of the spill. "Double bottoms could have reduced the Valdez spill by half," he said.

An internal Tanker Safety Study is another initiative being undertaken within the Office of Marine Safety, Security, and Environmental Protection. This study will look at existing and new construction vessels, both foreign and domestic. Plans will be considered for intensifying tanker inspection programs to exercise greater control over ships coming into U.S. ports—higher risk ships will be excluded from our waters.

While the interest in environmental issues caused by the Valdez incident created opportunities, there are also clear dangers for the Coast Guard in Congress' reaction. If the array of initiatives is enacted without sufficient funding, the Coast Guard will be faced with limited alternatives for reprogramming operating funds. Manpower costs currently account for two-thirds of the operating budget. The remaining one-third goes for maintaining and operating aircraft, cutters, and shore stations. Spare parts inventories already have suffered during previously lean budget years.

Law enforcement is the only mission area from which enough funds could be reprogrammed to pay for new environmental protection initiatives without posing an *immediate* threat to safety of life and property. The Coast Guard would have no choice but to once again reduce the level of its drug interdiction operations; and not all legislators are committed to funding the war on drugs if it detracts from important issues of local concern.

The Changing Drug War

A northbound aircraft appeared on the radar scope as it came through the Windward Passage between Cuba and Haiti on 17 July 1989. A "sensor bird" acquired the target and began tracking at 3:45 P.M. An hour later, a U.S. Army UH-60A helicopter was launched from Georgetown, Great Exuma, in the Bahamas with a U.S. Drug Enforcement Administration (DEA) agent and a Bahamian Drug Enforcement Unit (DEU) agent aboard. Twenty minutes later, a U.S. Coast Guard HH-3F helicopter lifted off from Nassau, New Providence, with a similar international drug team aboard. A second Coast Guard helicopter and team was launched from Freeport, Grand Bahama Island, 40 minutes later.

The "sensor bird" tracked the suspect aircraft northwest across the length of the Bahama Island chain. The helicopters kept out of sight as they moved north with the suspect. The suspicious aircraft finally rendezvoused with two speedboats at the northwest end of the Little Bahama Bank at 6:55 P.M. The plane circled and dropped its cargo of drugs to the boats waiting a few miles south of the Matanilla Shoal lighted buoy.

As the helicopters closed in, the boats fled at high speed and soon were lost. Packages of marijuana were found floating at the drop site. One of the boats later was seized by a Coast Guard Law Enforcement Detachment (LEDET) embarked aboard a U.S. Navy ship; the one person aboard was arrested. The drug plane landed at Hibiscus, FL, where the pilots abandoned their aircraft and escaped into the brush in the darkness.

This OPBAT (Operation Bahamas and Turks and Caicos Islands) case demonstrates the level of international and interagency cooperation being employed in drug interdiction today. Unfortunately, it also indicates the number of costly resources required to frustrate the delivery of one small shipment of drugs and the difficulty in apprehending the drug runners.

Rear Adm. Walter T. Leland, Coast Guard's Chief of Law Enforcement, said two important near-term issues face the Coast Guard in the drug-interdiction business. First is the service's role in helping to implement the President's National War on Drugs, and second, the impact of naming the Department of Defense as the lead agency for detecting and tracking drug shipments under the Anti-Drug Abuse Act (ADAA) of 1988.

WE CAN SOLVE YOUR PROBLEMS LATER

2010

2005

2000

1990

... OR HELP YOU AVOID THEM NOW

Long recognized as a premier problem solving organization, BDM wants you to know about something we do even better. We help you *avoid* many of tomorrow's problems (or at least minimize them) by making better choices, finding better answers, designing better systems ... today.

For example, BDM is creating millions of lines of software which is at the heart of a huge logistics information management system. This software is virtually error-free *by design* to avoid costly error correction and other problems later. For NASA, BDM's Risk Analysis and Management System (BRAMS) will provide an integrated assessment of technical, schedule, and resource risks associated with Space Station Freedom ... in time to do something about them. And the innovative computer/communications, information, and manufacturing systems we develop and integrate for other clients will not only meet today's requirements

but evolve easily and affordably to meet tomorrow's. In our test and evaluation work, too, we help clients achieve more effective, reliable systems in the first place, systems that won't have to undergo costly future fixes.

Faced with a serious problem today? We'll find superior solutions for you. We do it every day for clients in the defense community, civil government, and industry. We apply (and in many cases devise) the most modern tools of research, analysis, assessment, design, engineering, integration, testing, and training. Guided by the most effective tool of all, the human mind: BDM people.

BDM makes things work. Put us to work for you. To keep a problem from happening, or solve it if it does.
BDM International, Inc., 7915 Jones Branch Dr., McLean, Va. 22102. (703) 848-5000.

BDM

Ford A Ford Aerospace Company

The United States' inability to solve the drug problem at the borders has become painfully obvious during the past decade. But we cannot allow our borders to be routinely violated by criminal elements flooding the country with drugs—it is a matter of national integrity. "We've got to continue working at all levels to interdict and disrupt the flow of drugs into the country," Leland said. "A solid credible effort has to be made to interdict. . . . The current cost of the nation's interdiction efforts is estimated at $2.5 billion a year. That price will have to go up significantly if we're to be successful."

Smugglers' methods of delivering drugs to the United States have become increasingly sophisticated over the past 15 years, complicating interdiction efforts. In the 1970s large bulk shipments of marijuana were loaded into coastal freighters and fishing boats and sent north. The vessels, stateless or of foreign registry, sailed with impunity to the southern United States. The "mother ships," as they were called, waited in international waters beyond the jurisdiction of the Coast Guard and transferred their cargoes to small, fast pickup boats at prearranged times and rendezvous points. The boats then disappeared into any of the hundreds of coves and inlets along the U.S. coast or mingled with innocent traffic going into port.

The use of "mother ships" declined as international cooperation and reinterpretations of U.S. laws made hovering ships subject to seizure in international waters. In the early 1980s, drug smugglers avoided patrolling cutters by transporting bulk shipments of marijuana and some cocaine in cargo planes. The aircraft landed at clandestine air strips in the United States, where the bales of marijuana were transferred to waiting trucks. Then the planes, many leased or stolen, often were abandoned. As local police and federal agents began keeping a closer watch on small unmanned airstrips, it became more difficult for drug planes to land and be offloaded without being detected.

The preference of drug users for cocaine in the second half of the decade made smaller-volume air shipments more profitable with less risk of being caught. The drug smugglers began using air drops of floatable packages of narcotics to fast boats waiting just outside the U.S. waters or in the Bahamas. This type of delivery is extremely difficult to defend against. The air drop and pickup take only a matter of minutes and then the boats are gone. The aircraft, which never enters U.S. air space, returns to South America or one of the islands to avoid being seized. To stop this type of delivery requires a large investment in costly resources. And then, as shown in the actual case described, seizing the aircraft and boats and arresting the smugglers is a matter of luck. Coast Guard, DEA, and Customs Service operations have been successful in frustrating air deliveries, but not many arrests and seizures have resulted.

As Drug Policy Director William Bennet looks at where to invest his limited resources in the war on drugs, the efficiency of interdiction operations undoubtedly will be reviewed. The Coast Guard Commandant, Adm. Paul A. Yost, said in an interview for this essay, "Twenty-five percent of Coast Guard assets in terms of personnel, cutters, aircraft, everything, is devoted to drug interdiction. What happens if the decision is made to take funds from interdiction efforts and put them into other drug programs like eradication? We have to be careful how we handle our investments in interdiction. We've been robbing from other missions to finance drug operations. We have other programs such as fisheries enforcement and pollution enforcement that need resources. . . . We have to match Coast Guard efforts to the needs of the country."

After Cuba announced its intention to shoot down planes carrying drugs in the two air corridors across the island nation, narcotics traffic dropped drastically. Leaders in the United States will have to decide how serious they are about waging a war on drugs and make some tough decisions about the use of force. More forceful tactics are necessary to keep pace with the smugglers' changing delivery methods. As drugs become recognized as a threat to national security, the current rules of engagement and control of air access to the United States will have to be reviewed. Risks to flight safety will have to be weighed against potential benefits in controlling the air traffic that delivers the drugs.

Border surveillance is essential in any plan to control the entry of drugs into the country. A system of airborne radars, mounted in surface tethered balloons called aerostats, is being completed. When finished, the system will provide coverage from the Bahamas west across the Florida Straits, along the Gulf Coast to Brownsville, TX, then along the land border with Mexico. Funds for the aerostat fence have been appropriated and installations are coming on line. For years aerostats have operated effectively both on shore and at sea. Leland observed, "Aerostats are the best tool for the money for detection. Once the whole system is completed, results should be even better." The Coast Guard's mobile system of five sea-based aerostats will continue to provide data to patrolling cutters and planes. The wide-area, high-resolution radars mounted under balloons are effective in sorting out targets in the choke points between the islands. The weakness of aerostats is their vulnerability to bad weather. The systems have to be retrieved when high winds are predicted.

Aerostat data is provided to the jointly operated Coast Guard/Customs Service Command, Control, Communications, and Intelligence (C^3I) Center East, located in south Florida. At the dedication of the $33 million facility last April, President Bush said, "Think of this as . . . our early warning network against narcotics." The C^3I Center will collect and process data from civilian and defense radars and provide enforce-

Two-thirds of the earth is covered by Electric Boat.

For ninety years, Electric Boat has dedicated itself to overcoming one obstacle. The 360,000,000 cubic miles that make up the world's oceans.

That goal has led us to design and build submarines that are more efficient, more cost effective and more capable than ever thought possible.

Today, we're taking submarine technology even further. Computer-aided design. Automated hull fabrication. Modular construction. Artificial intelligence.

Perhaps that's why nearly two-thirds of American submarines out there are Electric Boats.

Error margin zero.

There's no room for error for decision-makers out there on the line. Their decisions depend on reliable military hardware that must accommodate a profusion of data from widely divergent sources and translate that data into intelligible, useful information. In real time.

With over 11,000 militarized processors delivered, Control Data goes beyond one architecture or one technology. We offer what *you need*, not what *we have*.

For example, Control Data can readily meet your needs with 16- or 32-bit designs in CISC or RISC protocols, using VHSIC technology, meeting required MIL-specs with a fluency in Ada. If you want to save your current applications software, we can emulate your present instruction set. Or we can optimize both hardware and software for your application.

For information on our capabilities, call 612/853-5000. Or write Control Data's Government Systems Group, P.O. Box O, HQF500, Minneapolis, MN 55440.

When it's your decision, Control Data.

$\boxdot$ CONTROL DATA

ment agencies with instant access to air and marine smuggling information. Intelligence and technology may be the keys to success in the country's antidrug operations; advances are steadily being made in both areas.

Coast Guard Law Enforcement Detachments (LEDET) embarked on Navy ships have proven to be highly successful, cost-effective tools in the drug war. Forty-one primary and 33 secondary teams of five to seven members sail aboard Navy ships operating in waters used by drug smugglers. The teams use the Navy ships as platforms from which to exercise their federal law enforcement authority. Since operations began in late 1982, Navy ships have accounted for the seizure of more than 850,000 pounds of marijuana and 2,000 pounds of cocaine, and arrests of 400 persons by LEDETs.

Narcotics smuggling is a high-profit, dynamic business driven by supply, demand, and risk factors. Violence, flowing from the drug cartels of Columbia and the drug posses of Jamaica, has become an integral part of the business. Organizations, from kingpins down to street dealers, will continue to cultivate markets anywhere and in any way they can. They will modify their tactics and methods to supply the demands of American markets. United States interdiction efforts must be equally imaginative and dynamic in responding to the crisis.

Personnel, Programs, and Appropriations

"Personnel are central to the organization," according to Rear Adm. George D. Passmore, Coast Guard's

■ *More of this kind of fast coastal interceptor definitely will be a requirement for the Coast Guard as the war against drug interdiction intensifies.*

Chief of Personnel and Training. "They are the oil that makes the machine work at its optimum." Unfortunately, the Coast Guard's oil may be getting a little thin. Service missions and workload continue to expand while the workforce remains the same, or even declines.

There is little doubt that Coast Guard men and women are the strength of the organization. They are also its greatest expense, consuming 60 percent of operating funds. Formal training programs add another 10 percent, with 12 percent of the workforce in classrooms at any given time. The 1990 personnel price tag is $1.035 billion and will get larger as the Coast Guard faces escalating personnel problems in the next few years.

A major organizational realignment was completed in 1988. Jobs at support units were combined, centralized, or eliminated to shift people from staff positions into operational billets. The objective was to reduce personnel in support functions by 25 percent. To accomplish that, two of the Coast Guard's 12 districts were eliminated—facilities, functions, and geographical responsibilities were absorbed by "flags" in adjacent districts. Support billets and operating funds then were taken from remaining districts to establish two regional Maintenance and Logistics Centers (MLC), one on each coast; MLCs were critical to the success of the reorganization. Atlantic and

Pacific Area Commanders next assumed operational and administrative control for all cutters larger than 180 feet. And finally, the Coast Guard's Washington headquarters was reorganized to combine and eliminate staff functions.

The realignment was projected to generate up to 1,000 billets for reassignment to the field, providing crews for new 270-foot medium endurance cutters, 110-foot Island class patrol boats, and an additional numbers for FRAM 378-foot high endurance cutters, as well as more crews and maintenance personnel for additional C-130, HU-25, and E2C aircraft. In considering the reorganization, Yost said, "The MLCs are providing services as good or better in all areas with the possible exception of naval engineering and contracting. . . . We have to tweak the new organization after it has had a chance to work, to make it as effective as possible." This will be one of Yost's objectives during his last year as Commandant.

The loss of flexibility was a negative aspect of the reorganization—a great deal of the Coast Guard's surge capability was wrung out of the system. Responses to a future crisis or unexpected missions will require additional personnel or the discontinuation of programs. According to Yost, "The reorganization doesn't hurt our surge capability as much as A76 [OMB's program to eliminate military billets by having service functions done by commercial organizations]. We have cooperated as A76 has methodically drawn down on our flexibility. It's time to slow A76 in the Coast Guard. We're losing our surge capability, distorting rating pyramids, and creating sea-shore rotation problems. I will petition OMB to cut the Coast Guard some slack!"

The realignment, while transferring more positions to field units, did little to correct the serious problem of vacant billets created by personnel shortages. Vacant billets are a growing problem aggravated by budget machinations, and not by the inability of the Coast Guard to recruit more people. It has been OMB's policy that the Coast Guard absorb up to one-half of the cost of personnel pay raises. To meet this unfunded obligation, the service has two alternatives: reprogram money from operations, or leave billets vacant to save on pay and allowances. In the past, a combination of the two approaches was used. A percentage of the nonsalary cost-of-living adjustments that were included in the budgets for Coast Guard field units—money that enables units to continue operations at the same level as the previous year—was not distributed. Withheld funds were used to cover part of the pay raise obligation. The rest was made up by intentionally leaving billets vacant. The result: reduced manpower, diminished spare parts, deferred maintenance, and curtailed operations. The cumulative effect on the personnel system was manning below authorized strength; the 1989 deficiency in personnel funds was $46 million.

Undermanning is a problem the Coast Guard must

address; the service cannot operate to its full potential when below strength. The incremental negative impacts of vacancies, spread servicewide, are deferred and not obvious. But, in reality, they represent lost opportunities for missions such as drug interdiction and environmental protection. A higher priority has to be put on manning to strength and filling billets.

The Coast Guard also will have to adjust to the changing nature and composition of its workforce. The percentage of seamen (E-3) now married, as compared to 10 years ago, has shot up from 7 percent to 38 percent, and 13 percent of all recruits entering the service have dependents. The costs of dependency and family support programs are becoming substantial. Requirements for family housing, health care, day care, and counseling services have increased dramatically. Surviving in high-cost, coastal recreational areas without government housing is a serious problem for young Coast Guard families. Cost-of-living indices are based on large areas and do not reflect the actual costs in local resort areas. Growing numbers of dual-income families, intraservice and interservice marriages, and single parents create assignment problems.

A dilemma facing the Coast Guard, and indeed all the armed forces, is the declining pool of eligible recruits. The U.S. population in age group 18-24 dropped from 30 million in 1979 to 28 million in 1986.

■ *One of the nation's only two oceangoing icebreakers makes its way through relatively thin ice. Recognizing the need for additional ships of this kind, Congress included $329 million in the FY 1990 defense budget for construction of one more.*

will have to consider remedial training programs to qualify candidates to enter basic petty officer schools. Curricula of schools also will have to be adjusted to accommodate less qualified recruits. Regardless of the alternatives used to compensate for less qualified entrants, they all will translate into greater costs and drain more people from the field.

The traditional multimission nature of the Coast Guard's workforce may have to be reevaluated as programs become more technical. Are mission requirements becoming too complex for a service of "generalists?" Most cutters, aircraft, and shore units are traditionally ready to respond to a variety of missions while performing in a primary program. Multimission flexibility always has been a source of pride for the Coast Guard—and possibly a "security blanket" for the integrity of the service. Will the time come when Coast Guard training, equipment, and mission needs become so specialized that the "general duty" concept is no longer viable? Perhaps, but for the foreseeable future, it appears that the Coast Guard will continue to rely on its people to adapt and respond to broad mission environments and needs—as they have for the past 200 years.

Senator Ernest F. Hollings (D-SC), Chairman of the Commerce, Science, and Transportation Committee, which oversees the Coast Guard, addressed the need to adequately fund the service during reauthorization hearings:

> The Valdez oil spill serves as a chilling reminder that we must have a strong and efficient U.S. Coast Guard in order to protect our citizens and our country. This 5th arm of our national defense must be equally equipped to handle anything from search and rescue for the weekend boater to the complex clean-up task caused by massive oil spills. The Coast Guard also plays a crucial role in our fight to stop the flow of illegal drugs into this country. We cannot afford to wait for the next disaster—we must support the Coast Guard now.

While senators and representatives recognize the Coast Guard's need for funds and express support, they are faced with the reality of the budget deficit. Restrained growth in government has resulted in strong competition among agencies for available funds. The large number of missions the Coast Guard performs results in a varied constituency of diverse interests and dispersed political influence. While no one denies the important role of the Coast Guard, funding support, particularly for "large ticket" items, is not always forthcoming.

Discouraged, Yost said, "There is no support in the authorization or appropriations committees of either the Senate or the House for a polar icebreaker. We need at least two more icebreakers but we can't get authorization or appropriations. We can't perform vital peacetime and wartime missions with less than four icebreakers. We'll have to have an emergency or a crisis before we'll get support."

By the year 2000, the figure is projected to be 25.2 million. While the recruit population is getting smaller, the overall quality of applicants also is declining.

The Coast Guard has obtained the limited number of recruits needed during recent no-growth years without much effort; young people always have been attracted by the service's missions. High first-term reenlistment rates, over 60 percent since 1985, also have decreased the need for accessions. Consequently, fewer recruiters and a smaller recruiting infrastructure were adequate to meet requirements. As demographics change, however, and equipment and systems become more complex, competition among armed forces for the smaller number of quality recruit candidates will become intense. Colleges, industry, and federal agencies also will be competing for resources from this pool. The Coast Guard simply will have to divert more resources, both personnel and dollars, from other programs into recruiting. Concludes Passmore, "We'll have to expand our scope of candidates."

In addition to increased expenditures recruiting, more training funds will be needed. Sophisticated hardware and operating systems will require more technical and longer training programs. The overall quality of education in the United States does not appear to be keeping pace with service demands. To cope with education deficiencies, the Coast Guard

But in a surprising last-minute development, Congress amended the defense appropriations bill to include funds for the Navy to build one polar icebreaker. It provided $329 million for that purpose. During consideration of defense appropriations legislation the chairman of the Defense Subcommittee of the Senate Appropriations Committee, Daniel Inouye (D-HI), had sought to have funds included for two icebreakers; however, Congress finally elected to fund only one.

The funding arrangement certainly overcomes the objections of critics of proposals to have the Coast Guard build icebreakers. Representative W.J. Tauzin (D-LA), chairman of the Coast Guard Subcommittee of the House Merchant Marine and Fisheries Committee, had said, "The primary mission of the polar icebreaker is defense support. The military character of this vessel justifies funding from defense funds rather than Coast Guard funds."

The Coast Guard operates and maintains the largest Aids-to-Navigation (ATON) system in the world—and does it with the oldest fleet of ships in the world. With a potential cost of $1 billion, the program for replacing aging oceangoing (WLB) and coastal (WLM) buoy tenders has come under close scrutiny. Twenty-seven of the original 39 Cactus class, oceangoing 180-foot WLBs built during World War II are still in operation. Renovations beginning in 1973 have kept the 45-year-old ships functioning. Considering the lead time for construction, however, one has to wonder if the old "work horses" will last until 1995, the earliest a new class could come on line.

Yost thinks the issue of replacement Coast Guard WLBs has been resolved. He said, "We are going to build the WLBs." When asked why money for the buoy tenders had dropped out of the budget, he replied, "Funds were not included in the FY 1991 budget because we're not sure of the design. We may include some oil-skimming capability in the vessels." Perhaps capabilities demonstrated by oceangoing tenders during the Valdez oil spill cleanup helped tip the scale in convincing the administration and Congress of the need for the multimission ships. Only 58 percent of WLB efforts are devoted to accomplishing aids-to-navigation work; the rest of the time they are involved in rescue work, law enforcement, domestic icebreaking, environmental protection, or military readiness. WLBs were involved in the Cuban boatlift, supported the military operation in Grenada, and are routinely used for emergencies such as hurricane recovery. Their lift capability makes them attractive for Maritime Defense Zone (MDZ) operations.

Construction of new coastal buoy tenders (WLM) also appears to have withstood the threat of "privatization." Yost said, "Privatization will not affect ships (WLB and WLM buoy tenders). That will be on the shore side (of ATON). The support and supply end. The environment is very good for the construction of buoy tenders."

In FY 1989, the Department of Defense transferred $200 million to the Coast Guard for defense-related expenditures, $140 million for "service-in-kind" (technical support, supplies, fuel, ammunition, etc.), and $60 million in cash. DOD said it could not continue to bail out the Coast Guard with funds but, then again in FY 1990, $140 million for "service in kind" and $160 million in cash were to be transferred to Coast Guard accounts. DOD bailouts are a mixed blessing: They provide immediate funds to operate, but they do not increase the Coast Guard's base for future-year funding. Appropriation committees have become reluctant to include defense-related money in the Coast Guard budget within the Department of Transportation Function 400, for fear it will be used to offset the cost of other transportation programs. Budgetary maneuvering distorts the appropriation process and raises questions as to whether the Coast Guard will ever be fully funded within the Department of Transportation.

The Coast Guard was created 200 years ago to solve a problem. Large foreign debts from the Revolutionary War had to be repaid—but, in 1789, the country's treasury was almost empty. Congress passed a law setting tariffs on imported goods to raise revenues to service the debt and fund the operation of the government. Alexander Hamilton, first Secretary of the Treasury, realized that efforts to collect tariffs would be futile without the power to force shippers, long accustomed to smuggling goods past the British, to comply. At Hamilton's request, the first Congress authorized creation of a seagoing armed service to enforce the revenue laws vital to the survival of the struggling new nation. Ten ships were built, an officer corps commissioned, and crews enlisted; most of the officers and men were experienced, having fought against the British at sea during the War. Once outfitted and armed, the ships put to sea as the Revenue Cutter Service, the country's only armed force afloat. They were the beginning of today's Coast Guard.

Two centuries later, the Coast Guard still is responding to national problems. The service's 38,000 men and women operate 257 cutters, 229 aircraft, and a system of hundreds of shore facilities in this country and abroad. The Coast Guard ranks as the twelfth largest naval force in the world. Service missions have expanded well beyond the original collection of revenue for the Treasury. Today's Coast Guard enforces a wide range of federal laws, protects life and property on the water, preserves the marine environment and, by Act of Congress, ". . . is a branch of the Armed Forces of the United States at all times." The Coast Guard continually trains and exercises with the country's other armed forces to maintain its readiness to engage in defense operations. The service's flexibility to respond to changing missions is recognized as a major strength and lends credence to its motto: *Semper Paratus— Always Ready.*

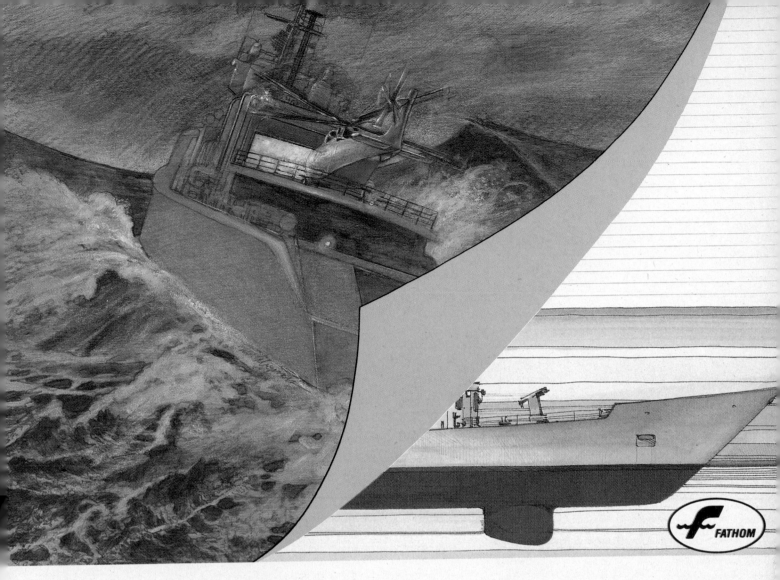

Introducing a new chapter in ASW support from Indal Technologies

For more than 30 years, navies and coast guards around the world have relied on Indal Technologies for a complete range of shipborne helicopter support systems.

This capability has recently been expanded with the acquisition of Fathom Oceanology, a world leader with more than 20 years in the design, manufacture and support of sonar cable handling systems, towed vehicles and other sophisticated underwater technologies.

Indal's experience in fully-integrated helicopter recovery and deck handling systems, telescopic hangars and hangar doors has given the company a unique place among those who operate their helicopters in the world's most demanding flying environment — at sea.

Now, one company provides the expertise for ASW operations support, from the sky to beneath the surface. It's a new depth of capability that offers navies and coast guards a single source for ASW support.

This is the first page of a new chapter which begins with 50 years of blue-water experience.

INDAL TECHNOLOGIES

Indal Technologies Inc.
3570 Hawkestone Rd.
Mississauga, Ontario L5C 2V8 Canada
Tel: (416) 275-5300 FAX: (416) 273-7004
Toll-free in the U.S. only: 1-800-263-7340

Despite Perestroika, Soviet Naval Capability Continues to be Formidable

"The United States seethes with ethnic unrest. In the northwest states thus far it has been largely peaceful. Elsewhere it has been violent. There have been bloody clashes between WASPS and Hispanics and murderous skirmishes between Afro-Asians and Chinese. At the same time, in Georgia, nationalist demonstrations have provoked brutal reactions from internal security forces. Among the countries of Western Europe, the sense of an Atlantic Alliance in decline is even sharper. Individual governments are increasingly going their own way."

Not true. But substitute Soviet Union for United States, Baltic republics for northwest states, Armenians and Azerbaijanis for WASPS and Hispanics, Uzbeks and Turks for Afro-Asians and Chinese, and truth is restored. Only Georgia needs no change of name, and for Europe West, read Europe East.

In a narrow sense the internal political affairs of the USSR are not the concern of the Western military establishment, unless in some way they directly affect our ability to defend ourselves. Yet, in spite of the absolute uncertainty as to what happens next in Soviet affairs, the process of Western disarmament can be said to have already started. Public pressure is growing for cutbacks in defense budgets, and the sense of purpose of the armed forces is beginning to be undermined. If you find that statement hard to

By RICHARD SHARPE

CAPTAIN RICHARD SHARPE succeeded Captain John E. Moore in 1987 as editor of *Jane's Fighting Ships* upon retirement from the Royal Navy. His distinguished career included command of both submarines and surface ships and considerable duty in the intelligence community.

take, try asking the recruiters. In other words, we already are affected, but only because we choose to be.

If the United States was in fact suffering the internal unrest described above, there would not be much sympathy with the view that White House policies were responsible as part of a deep-laid plot to undermine the security of the Warsaw Pact! And yet, in all seriousness, there are those in the Western military who see *perestroika* as part of a long-term plan to disarm and disrupt the cohesion of the West while rebuilding the Soviet industrial base for the ultimate construction of bigger and better ships, tanks, and aircraft. In other words, *perestroika* is merely a euphemism for *peredyshka*, which means taking time out to restructure the technology base, to use military management to improve civilian industrial efficiency, to charm, lie, suborn, and steal from the West so that, at some time in the future, Soviet technology can compete on more equal terms. That may well be the effect if we allow ourselves to be disarmed by the natural optimism of those who want to believe that all is now benign in superpower relationships. Even the proponents of the most optimistic interpretation of Gorbachev's reforms have to admit that there is a list of other outcomes to the Soviet modern-day convulsions, stretching from the total disintegration of the empire at one end of the scale to the speedy restoration of a latter-day Stalin at the other. Furthermore, some of the many options in between those two extremes will remain a possibility for years to come, and a few may even come about sequentially.

Therefore, what should matter in the military analysis is that we leave watching the man's lips to the media, assessing his intentions to the academics and those whose unenviable function is to find a coherent plan or strategy behind the pragmatism, and focus on the more simple task, which is to measure the capabilities with clear-eyed objectivity—and the options such capabilities bestow upon the owner. Put like that, you could say that in naval hardware terms, not much has changed. The policy of reasonable sufficiency is "full of sound and fury, signifying nothing."

Can the Soviet SSBNs still carry out a first or second strategic strike that would lay waste to the United States? No problem. Can her attack submarines, backed by acoustic disruption and sabotage of relevant shore establishments, deploy to positions where they could destroy economic and reinforcement shipping in the Atlantic and Pacific? No doubt at all.

THE COLOR OF PROGRESS.

LUCAS GREEN. UNIQUE.

SYSTEMS AT THE HEART OF THE WORLD'S

GREAT AIRCRAFT.

IN POWER GENERATION, FLIGHT

CONTROL AND ENGINE MANAGEMENT

LUCAS' COMMITMENT TO ITS PARTNERS

IS TOTAL.

OUR COLOR FLIES WITH THE LATEST

BOEING, THE OSPREY, THE AIRBUS, THE

C17, THE TORNADO, THE EH101 AND

MANY LEADING AEROSPACE PROJECTS

THROUGHOUT THE WORLD.

TO THOSE WHO PURSUE EXCELLENCE,

THERE IS ONE COLOR. LUCAS GREEN.

THE ART OF AEROSPACE, THE WORLD OVER.

HEAD OFFICES IN **Lucas Aerospace**

BRITAIN 021 704 5171, USA 703 264 1704,

FRANCE 1 45 61 95 25.

Could a combination of submarine, merchant ship, and air-launched modern mines effectively blockade most of the free world's major harbors and narrow seas? Almost certainly. Could invasion forces concentrated on the flanks of NATO Europe, around Japan, or even in the Arabian Sea, successfully be supported by amphibious forces operating under land-based naval air cover? Difficult, but possible. Could the fleet as a whole take on worldwide deployments for the purpose of exerting political pressure through military presence in peacetime? The Politburo just needs to give the word.

In consequence, those in the West who are responsible for progress to a safer world argue that the only sensible way forward is arms control, balanced force reductions, confidence-building measures, intrusive verification, and a steady, mutual decline in new construction and modernization programs. A sort of reciprocal deterioration with force levels being maintained for defensive purposes only, and whatever is necessary for limited conflict and for coping with the unreasonable men of the Third World who have not yet reached that level of civilized sophistication that rejects war as an acceptable "diplomacy by other means."

The key question is: Does the Soviet Union negotiating team have the same objective clearness of purpose as its U.S. counterparts when it comes to arms control negotiations? The evidence, such as it is so far, is ambiguous, which is hardly surprising given the current levels of confusion in the Soviet evolutionary political process. Taking the gloomy view, what is certain is that since the end of World War II, the Soviets have visibly enjoyed the prestige of superpower summitry based solely on their military strength. In most other ways, this is a Third World nation with an almost 19th century standard of living for the vast majority of her people, major balance of payments problems, declining oil resources, a currency nobody wants, and an industrial base which, with the partial exception of the section supporting the space and military programs, maintains plants and practices that are decades out of date. Not a combination likely to encourage the total sacrifice by the ruling party of the military platform which provides the superpower status.

For those involved in commenting openly about developments in the Soviet Navy, this has been a mixed year for information-gathering. On the plus side, the Soviet naval hierarchy has been revealing more than before (not difficult) both to civilians like the U.S. House Armed Services Committee passing through Sevastopol last summer, as well as to the various military delegations to the USSR which have been reciprocated by Soviet senior officers visiting NATO countries. They have even been telling their own citizens much more than usual. In addition, for the first time in many years, there have been visits by ships of the U.S. and British fleets to the Soviet ports in the Black and Baltic Seas, and return visits to U.S.

and European harbors by Soviet units. Images of Adm. William J. Crowe Jr. (retired Chairman, U.S. Joint Chiefs of Staff) disappearing into the bowels of a Victor III class SSN, or Adm. V.N. Chernavin (Commander in Chief, Soviet Navy) at sea off Scotland in HMS Invincible have caused many seasoned cold-war veterans to blink in reassurance that this is not some sort of Colombian-induced mirage. And when experienced naval officers are allowed to chat, see the ships, and make first-hand assessments, some of the intelligence officers' mystique and guesswork becomes of less significance. It is said that the Queen believes that all buildings smell of fresh paint, and it was interesting to note Adm. Crowe's comment that whereas the Victor was obviously a working model, the battle cruiser *Kirov* had been "prepared" for the occasion. In the late 1960s, I remember going on board a Kynda-class cruiser which was open to visitors and noting that the elevating mechanism for the SSN 3B launcher was overpainted with several coats of high gloss. This particular missile system clearly had not been through "user checks" for months, probably years. There are those in the UK Portland sea-training organization who maintain that from a small boat at 50 yards on a dark night, they can sense a poorly prepared ship as she arrives to start working up; such a vessel exudes an air of incompetence. More obvious indicators will not have escaped Admirals Crowe and Chernavin and their staffs, or the sailors visiting Sevastopol, Leningrad, and Norfolk. Even if the sample size is small, such evidence can contribute much to a greater mutual understanding of likely capabilities.

In fact the senior Soviet visitor for the *Invincible* sea day was the Minister of Defense, General Dmitri Yazov, who at one stage indicated (to the obvious annoyance of his naval colleague) that he did not think much of the survivability of large surface ships. The inability of soldiers and airmen to grasp the enormity of the scale of the maritime battle seems to transcend international boundaries. Brief visits on sunny summer days in coastal regions is perhaps not the best way to educate them.

On the debt side of information gathering, the Pentagon's *Soviet Military Power* annual publication did not appear until September (six months later than usual) and in his first annual statement to Congress, the new Director of Naval Intelligence inevitably was more circumspect and less revealing of official thinking than his predecessor in 1988. *Soviet Military Power* has come in for some criticism in the past for its alleged overtly propagandist presentation, but it has been an invaluable source of facts, and the reader is always free to make up his own mind on both the analysis and the rhetoric. Regrettably, this year's edition is very short of new facts. In the endless and legitimate struggle between intelligence source protection and the needs of a better informed public, the pendulum is currently on the side of caution in detailed published statements. Not surprisingly, this has led to a greater release of unofficial and off-the-cuff statements as senior officers in Washington fight for public support for their procurement programs.

In mid-1989, the naval order of battle was, broadly speaking, as shown in the table reproduced from *Jane's Fighting Ships, 1989-90*, although in the six months since then the paying-off of older ships has accelerated.

Type	Northern	Baltic	Black Sea and Caspian	Pacific
SSBN	40	—	—	23
SSB	—	6	—	7
SSGN	30	—	—	22
SSG	7	3	2	4
SSN	58	—	—	27
SS*	40	30	25	30
CV	2	—	—	2
CHG	—	—	2	—
CGN	1	1	—	1
CG	10	1	6	11
DDG	16	9	13	14
FFG	8	6	7	11
CL	2	1	3	4
DD**	1	2	3	1
FF and FFL***	40	30	45	45
FAC(M) and Missile Corvettes	25	50	35	50
Light Forces	20	120	120	170
MCM Forces	60	120	80	100
LPD	—	—	—	2
LST	9	8	8	13
LSM	7	10	20	6
Hovercraft	10	25	20	25
Depot Repair and Support Ships	30	5	23	27
Underway Replenishment Ships	7	3	7	11
Support Tankers	10	6	7	8

 * In addition about 70 believed in reserve.
 ** In addition 10 "Kotlin" class and 5 "Skory" class in reserve.
 *** In addition about 15 believed in reserve.

Source: Jane's Fighting Ships, 1989-90

Changes to the warship construction program in the last 12 months have not been particularly significant if signs of fiscal restraint are what you are seeking. Typhoon and Delta IV SSBNs, Oscar II SSGNs, Akula, Sierra, and Victor III SSNs are all rolling programs producing an average construction rate of five to six hulls a year, to which can be added three to four Kilo-class diesel boats. This may be down from the peak years of when a submarine was launched every five or six weeks, but given the fire power and improved operational effectiveness of these modern classes, in no sense can it be construed as a cutback in the overall submarine program. Samples taken in any one calendar year can be also misleading, as they were when it was announced that only four nuclears were launched in 1988. A new class of SSGN or Oscar variant continues to be expected; its main role will be to carry the SSNX-24 long-range land-attack cruise missile. Yankee conversions to SSN/SSGN also are proceeding at about one to two per year. Norwegian and Danish defense spokesmen claim that the development of the Yankee class (in both original and converted forms) in the Norwegian Sea is filling the INF gap left by the withdrawal of ground-launched systems in Europe.

The aircraft carrier program is equally dynamic, with the fourth Kiev-class joining the fleet, two Tbilisi-class larger deck platforms either on sea trials or fitting out, and a class of perhaps four 75,000 ton carriers to come in the next decade. According to a Russian admiral, these new carriers will have conventional power plants, steam catapults, and squadrons of Flanker fighter aircraft. The fourth nuclear-powered Kirov-class battle cruiser was launched during the year, a fifth is building, and a follow-on design is forecast. A third Slava-class cruiser has been commissioned with another of the same or similar type still to come, and the established launch rates of the impressive missile destroyers of the Sovremenny and Udaloy classes show no signs of immediate change. The first of a new frigate class to follow the Krivak IIs for the Navy will be commissioned in 1990, and for the first time a Soviet naval frigate (as opposed to the KGB type), will have full helicopter facilities in common with most of the world's navies' modern ships in this category.

Where the "bean counters" will soon be able to point to is an undeniable decline in overall numbers, as classes of submarines and ships that long have outlived their operational usefulness join the queues for the breakers' yards, perhaps allowing the Soviets to claw back some precious foreign currency in the process. Twenty cruisers, destroyers, and frigates dating back to the early 1950s have been paid off for scrap in the last two years and many more, about 70 hulls, could be stricken without any real adverse impact on the fleet's fighting efficiency. In the same category are at least 23 nuclear submarines of the first generation HEN classes are coming up to their 30th birthdays, and over 100 ancient diesel boats, many of which have been in reserve for some years.

■ *The Soviet cruiser Slava, first of its class, was to host President Bush and President Gorbachev off Malta in December, but high seas prompted a change of location.*

The Soviets also have said that in 1990 they will remove the six Golf II-class SSBs stationed in the Baltic.

Getting rid of that lot should be classified as delayed natural wastage and not as a unilateral reduction in naval capabilities. Inroads need to be made into much newer hulls before there can be any suggestion of a debate on reciprocal cutbacks, and even then a balance would be extraordinarily hard to judge, given the different dependencies upon the sea of the two superpower alliances, and the extreme difficulties of, for instance, measuring how many disparate types of ASW units are the equivalent of one SSN.

As this huge tonnage of ancient metal is discarded it will release funds, sailors, and maintenance resources which can be used to make the Soviet fleets leaner and fitter with more effort going into training and manning those modern submarines and ships which are most able to perform effectively in today's maritime warfare environment. It might also help to alleviate the four fleet commanders' chronic submarine-waterspace-management problems.

Of course some will say that this is a typical military analysis—only a threat-production merchant could make a virtue of a declining order of battle. But, by their own admission, the Soviet admirals have been stretched too thin on manpower and resources for maintenance and the number of major surface ships and attack submarines in particular still looks too heavy for defensive purposes, even to the most credulous exponents of the defensive bastion theory of Soviet maritime power. Large-deck aircraft carriers, nuclear-powered battle cruisers, and attack submarines are not the sort of fleet units needed for day running from the Kola Peninsula. Nuclear propulsion is the optimum method of providing worldwide seagoing endurance, and, as the British discovered in the 1960s, it is not easy to make a convincing case for shipborne strike and air defense aircraft if the

staff requirement says you will only operate your surface ships within range of fighter aircraft based ashore. The Soviet naval staff must have difficulty in keeping straight faces when they read that their multi-million ruble carriers are assessed as being required to "extend the land-based air defense umbrella."

One recent and clever explanation for the narrow view that this is a fleet primarily designed for defense of the land mass flanks is that the analyses of Soviet procurement and operational strategies have been confused. A navy must have ships. Those who have worked in the ship procurement business know very well that the operational requirement for a new class of warship pays close attention to whatever is likely to be most acceptable to the transient civilians who make the final decisions within the confines and limits of the defense policy and military strategy which is in force at the time. The operational life of a ship from design to scrapyard is at least 30 to 40 years, sometimes more. By contrast the small print of policies and strategies is in a constant state of flux, and major changes are inevitable every few years. But once you have built the new ship, it can be used and adapted to meet directed tasks which were foreseen by the navy but which may not even have made the small print in the original requirement.

Then there is that potent operational symbol of the major navies known as "supporting the seaborne strategic deterrent." No matter how tenuous the link, no staff officer worth his salt will fail to insert it as part of the indispensable rationale for his new piece of kit. The bureaucracy of equipment procurement is a confrontational process of bringing together the vested interests and fashions of national defense and alliance sensibilities, industrial development and local politics, service morale and sales potential, perceptions of status, and international aspirations. To extrapolate the Soviet operational strategy from the resultant product requires an imaginative leap in the dark onto a moving platform. And if the procurement-policy decision-making process is shrouded in drifting mists, there are equal problems with the analysis of their operational patterns. The principle of exercising where you think you might have to fight is enshrined in Western naval thinking, but then so is the right of the individual to travel where he wishes. Communist regimes traditionally do not like letting people leave the homeland, and, in spite of some relaxations, recent events in East Germany and Moldavia have been a salutary reminder of the reason behind such repressive restrictions. So it should be no surprise that if such a mind-set is in force on land, the same mentality is at work at sea, only this time the boundaries are off North Cape, Bornholm Island, or the Kamchatka Peninsula. In spite of modern communications, naval command on the high seas has a whiff of bourgeois freedom which is the delight of sailors in the free world's navies, but is at odds with the whole tradition of a repressive and bureaucratic structure. So the conclusion is that both the procurement and the operational models are inadequate as indicators of the true Soviet maritime strategy and the only safe analysis is not "what are they *for*" but "what they can *do*, these submarines and ships." The answer should continue to cause serious concern to those nations whose economic and political well-being depends upon the free movement of trade at sea.

In many ways, operational deployments and developments have provided most of the major news stories in 1989.

In any warship, fire is an ever-present potential hazard and, apart from the sound of uncontrolled running water, nothing gets a submariner off his backside faster than the smell of burning. Even an innocuous looking smoldering rag in a bilge can fill a whole compartment with smoke almost in the time it takes to sound the alarm. And if you are dived how do you get rid of the smoke? The tendency towards greater automation, smaller crews, and therefore more unmanned spaces is bound to add to this hazard, and the Mike-class SSN *Komsomolets* sinking off Bear Island in April was the victim of just such a combination. The public piecing together of badly translated official statements and early Soviet media speculation has produced some fairly fanciful versions of the sequence of events, but there is not much doubt that a fire in an initially unmanned machinery space got out of control and containment attempts were frustrated by a high-pressure air leak within the compartment. It is then probable that smoke overcame the propulsion-plant watchkeepers, and the reactor was shut down with the consequent loss of the primary source of power. Breathing apparatus may allow people to survive smoke, but monitoring and controlling complex reactor, propulsion, and electrical distribution panels is a scary business if you cannot see more than a couple of inches in front of your face mask. The electrical load distribution system throughout the submarine also was badly affected, which would have degraded life support and fire fighting facilities. The last straw was when the built-in breathing system became contaminated. Having surfaced, and with a main hull hatch probably opened to allow the crew to escape to the casing, the submarine was almost bound to be lost. It is not clear whether flooding was caused primarily through the open hatch or hatches (a medium sea was running) or because the captain decided that it was the only way to put the fire out before primary nuclear systems containment was endangered, or because an explosion of high-pressure air or oxygen bottles in the vicinity of the fire fractured hull glands, or even the hull itself. It was probably a combination, but the captain going back into the control room at the last moment suggests scuttling could have been the final cause. The revelation of the detachable escape chamber, probably built-in at the back end of the sail, has

■ *Superb examples of the kinds of modern ships, submarines, and aircraft that make Soviet fighting forces so formidable are a Sovremennyy-class destroyer, the very quiet, extremely fast nuclear-powered attack submarine of the Akula class, and the MiG-29 Fulcrum.*

been something of a surprise to Western analysts, although reports of the releasing catches sticking in a five-year old hull has a ring of truth to it, as does the apparent failure of the venting mechanism as the capsule surfaced. It also was confirmed by Chernavin that this submarine was a prototype hull designed to dive to 1,000 meters.

There can be nothing but sympathy for those sailors who experienced every submariner's nightmare, and there will have been no smugness in Western nuclear submarine communities.

Sadly though, this event was followed in fairly quick time by two more incidents involving nuclear propulsion plant failures, one in an Alfa SSN and the second in an Echo II SSGN, although neither of these was a fatal accident. Once a year is bad luck, twice is a coincidence, three times means questions of competence begin to become a bit more pointed. Certainly one Soviet naval captain was in no doubt "nuclear reactor operators can cope with only 30 to 50 percent of what they should be capable of handling."

Most navies have a few senior officers who talk like that, but Defense Minister Yazov, when asked for his views on the spate of accidents, seemed to agree: "... technical deficiencies in various systems, mistakes of designers and shipbuilders, and an impermissibly lax attitude displayed by the Navy during the acceptance of submarines from industry. The system of naval personnel recruitment and training, and the organization and standards of equipment of the sea rescue service should evidently be upgraded." Not surprisingly, these comments were repeated and endorsed in the State Commission report on the sinking of the *Komsomolets*.

There always has been Western concern over Soviet nuclear-propulsion safety standards, and a belief that their submarines achieve faster speeds by operating their reactors outside the stringent safety "envelopes" applied by the United States and United Kingdom. If at the same time engineering standards and training skills also are suspect, adja-

cent countries like Norway and Japan have every right to be concerned. Tales of radiation-sickness problems associated with the first Indian Charlie-class SSGN leased from the Soviets also are not encouraging. With an eye to catching the media's attention, an Indian left-wing organization has even called it the Chernobyl class.

A more balanced view might be that, given the extraordinary numbers of submarines and the speed with which the Soviet fleet has built up in three decades, overall reliability and safety have been fairly good. Out of area the Soviets have now lost three nuclear submarines in the Atlantic and Norwegian Sea, and one diesel boat carrying ballistic missiles in the Pacific. Statistically, and given the numbers of hulls in each fleet, that overall record compares adequately with the U.S. Navy. The major difference is that Soviet fatal accidents have been more recent, and U.S. deployment levels are much greater in number.

Growing numbers of nuclear reactors and weapons on the seabed inevitably have raised the environmental issue of how long it might take for contamination to become a serious problem. There are divergent expert views, but, given the nature of reactor pressure vessels and reactor compartments, it seems unlikely that local radiation levels will ever rise above background ambient, although no one can object if the sunken hulls are occasionally monitored. Nuclear warheads, on the other hand, apparently have isotopes which, when they are eventually released by the break up of the weapon casing, are more likely to be detectable in the vicinity of the wreck. It would be nice to think that, at least where vertical-launch weapons are concerned, some design effort is being put into contingency methods of seabed recovery of the warheads, in the event of the submarine sinking in deep water.

Apart from these rather dramatic events, the Soviet Navy has had a quiescent year with warship deployment levels down by some 20 percent from 1988, although the pattern of operations, including submarines, continues much as before. A notable exception has been the reported slight increase in the research and spying effort by auxiliary naval vessels, particularly in the field of oceanography and hydrographic data gathering. From Iceland to the South Atlantic and from Alaska to the South Pacific, Soviet hydroacoustic-related research goes on throughout the year. Because such information is critical in submarine warfare, this is yet another (if one were needed) unambiguous indication that the strategic plan is not to keep most of their attack submarines in defensive bastions. At the same time, there is no doubt that warship fuel allocations have been drastically reduced, that expensive excursions in the cause of supporting Third World totalitarian states are now a low priority, and that large naval task forces roaming the oceans, which have never been the Soviet style, are construed as unhelpful in the business of projecting a new Soviet military strategy as one that is shifting to the defensive. The navy also has inadequate numbers of trained men and continues to be selective in the ships it sends out of area.

Much has been written recently on the prospects for naval arms control. But no serious agenda seems likely to be agreed to in the near future, except possibly on sea-launched cruise missiles, which is one of the more difficult verification issues. In 1912 the young Winston Churchill wrote that "in many ways the German Navy is to them more in the nature of a luxury. Our naval power involves British existence. A navy is existence for us; it is expansion to them." Put the U.S. Navy and its maritime allies on one side of the wire and the Warsaw Pact fleets on the other and, if anything, the point becomes even more valid today (although the use of the word "luxury" was considered ill-judged at the time). In such circumstances the Soviet call for naval hardware cutbacks and control of operating areas is both logical and predictable. It is therefore possible to sympathize

with the "Hell, no!" school of Western response to naval arms control and at the same time recognize that being totally negative is unhelpful in the struggle for international hearts and minds. The basis of the confidence-building measures being negotiated in Europe is to lessen the mutual fear of surprise attack on land. If that means searching for a way to inhibit those seaborne-theater weapon systems which could be used at very short notice against land targets, this does not seem to be too big a price to pay, if the alternative is what can all too easily be represented as irrational support of an obvious vested interest. Control measures that are verifiable and favor neither side are not going to be easy to find, but whereas the West can claim with justification its total dependence upon the sea and its navies, the same logic is not sufficiently elastic to embrace seaborne-theater land-attack weapon systems under all circumstances.

Away from home waters, the Soviet naval threat in 1990 resides predominantly in its modern nuclear submarine flotillas and mining stocks, although this may change in the coming years if the aircraft program maintains its present momentum—in spite of Yazov's reservations. By far the most vulnerable potential target for their attack submarines is economic and resupply shipping worldwide, and the major ports of exit and entry. If the Soviets are serious about naval confidence-building measures, they have got to reduce the threat. Because verification procedures are not up to monitoring submarine movements within imposed geographical limits at sea, only the curtailment of the construction programs and the reduction in numbers of modern operational attack submarine hulls meets this requirement. Nothing else should be allowed to affect Western investment in naval defense forces. But that should not stop us looking for other ways of showing goodwill to reduce the risk of confrontation at sea and ease the way towards long-term multilateral force reductions. For the moment, the best way of describing naval arms control is that of "a not very good idea whose time has not yet come."

Whatever develops next within the process of barely controlled radical change within the Soviet empire, the architects in Moscow (whoever they are) will have as their first priority the national interests of the Soviet Union. If the security of the free world benefits from the direction those interests take, it will be a great bonus, and may lead to more initiatives in the steady progress of arms control over which so much time has been spent to so little real effect in these last few years. Some of these initiatives are bound to try and include naval forces. But the political and military history of both Russia and the Soviet Union suggests the continuation of a considerable military power with ideals and politics far removed from Western democracy. Only when that power has been substantially reduced can we afford to relax our own efforts of maintaining peace through strength.

every project—a management emphasis on "no surprises," a reputation for bringing in projects on time, on budget, on spec.

And the same is true whether it's ASW, or self-protection, or C³, or simulation, or any of our other chosen areas.

Loral: It's a good synonym for *defense electronics.*

Loral digital autopilot controller enables Vertical Launch ASROC missile to find its target.

CAPTOR mine can sense and confirm a target and fire a torpedo.

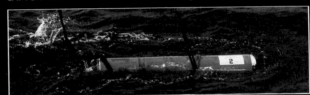

MK-30 training device simulates the "thumbprint" of adversary submarines.

VHSIC-based, fully militarized Associative Processor (ASPRO) allows real-time threat response.

We Must Maintain Security Posture We Now Enjoy In the Pacific

In "think tanks" and editorial board rooms, the standards of measurement for national security, in the Pacific and elsewhere, have changed. No longer can security be judged by the quality or quantity of military hardware or by the numbers of men and women in uniform. Today, with trade imbalances and debtor-nation status, economics, in the minds of many, dominates national security. Even the Soviets, it is argued, have discovered the folly of maintaining a first rate military with a faltering economy.

On the political side, the tremendous change occurring in the Soviet Union and her warming relationship with the United States allow resolution of differences without direct involvement of military forces. Defense dollars can be diverted to schools, the homeless, the war on drugs, and other noble causes. It seems logical to conclude that in the better world that is dawning, future battle will be between diplomats and economists, not warriors. Such thinking is not only simplistic, but it is also wrong. It is still a dangerous world out there!

There always has been an economic and political dimension to national security, but neither has domi-

By THOMAS B. HAYWARD and RONALD J. HAYS

ADMIRAL THOMAS B. HAYWARD commanded the Seventh Fleet in the Far East and the Pacific Fleet before becoming Chief of Naval Operations in 1978. He retired from the Navy in 1982 and now heads his own Honolulu-based consulting firm on Asia/Pacific matters. He travels extensively throughout that vast area. ADMIRAL RONALD J. HAYS served successively as Vice Chief of Naval Operations and as Commander in Chief, U.S. Pacific Command before retiring in 1988. He now is president and chief executive officer of a Honolulu-based center for high technology research.

nated. Since World War II, the military, with results that impress, has been the dominant factor in national security. U.S. Pacific forces have kept the peace in the Pacific and satisfied U.S. security interests. U.S. Pacific forces have created the environment that allowed nations of the Pacific to prosper, both economically and politically. And U.S. Pacific forces, along with increasingly capable Asian forces, will be needed to satisfy our security interest in the future, notwithstanding conventional wisdom about the overwhelming role of economics.

Pacific leaders are mindful of our changing views about the nature of security, and tend to worry about the meaning of change at a time when the geostrategic equation throughout the region is shifting. Few will question that the presence of U.S. military forces has been the anchor for Asia's strategic balance for four decades, yet today few will question that U.S. and Soviet influence have declined. Japan, South Korea, China, Australia, and India increasingly exercise economic, political, and military muscle within the region. At the same time, there is anxiety about whether economic factors will jeopardize friendly relations, security treaties, or U.S. military presence in the Western Pacific.

The level of anxiety is revealed when Japanese or Korean friends begin a discussion on how to protect a superb military-to-military relationship by avoidance of sticky economic issues. "Let's stick to purely military matters" is the suggestion. The idea has merit for the trenches, but, of course, economics cannot be avoided at the national leadership level; neither can unpleasant political issues such as human rights or crooked politics. Thus, when dealing with international security matters, whether we like it or not, there is an inseparable trio of economics, politics, and the military.

The challenge of national security is to maintain the proper balance among the three elements. Unfortunately, circumstances do not favor balance. Take, for example, the Japanese FSX fighter debate or the "son of FSX" issue with Korea. One would expect quick endorsement of a declared intent by an ally to build a new, more capable fighter aircraft that can serve mutual defense interest. Such has not happened nor, short of war, is it likely to happen ever again where high technology transfer, competition in world markets, and trade imbalances are involved. It is well accepted that technology developments can capture the marketplace and that important technology derives from military hardware. Accordingly, eco-

nomics, rather than military posture, can become the dominant factor in deciding national security issues—an ominous development.

Anxiety about our budget and trade deficits and credit for improving relations with the Soviets notwithstanding, we need to maintain the security posture that we now enjoy in the Pacific. The region is too important to the future of the United States to "bet on the come" for a more perfect world and phase out large segments of the force structure. Ask our friends and allies, and they will say that removal of the forward deployed U.S. Pacific forces would create an unstabilizing power vacuum that others will try to fill.

Former Ambassador Mike Mansfield's prediction about the "Pacific Century" is likely to come to pass. Sixty percent of the world's population already is there; some of the world's largest armies are there; 18 of the 20 largest banks in the world are in Japan; robotic manufacturing is proliferating; trans-Pacific trade now exceeds trans-Atlantic trade; political dynamism grows, and rapid change has become the norm. If all these facts are unconvincing, it might be pointed out that the area for potential economic development in the U.S. tripled with the Presidential proclamation of a 200-nautical-mile exclusive economic zone. Much of that increase occurred in the Pacific.

With an abundance of human and natural resources, the potential for the Pacific is virtually unlimited, but it is also a region of vast diversity and volatility. Friction from overlapping interests is inevitable. It is a region with latent problems, running the gamut from border disputes to oppressive regimes. Nevertheless, on balance the region can be viewed quite correctly as a success story. Regional security from the U.S. perspective is in fair shape, but by no means can it be taken for granted.

In all modesty, the successes that are found in the Pacific are attributable in many ways to the United States. First, we provided a protective security umbrella that allowed nations to look inward to their own political and economic development without concern for external threat. Secondly, as nations developed a manufacturing base, we opened our markets for their goods. The results in many Asian countries have been spectacular, but the results also are the seeds of economic problems we now face.

The bedrock of our security interests in the Pacific are the mutual security treaties and friendly relationships with "western" minded nations. There are five formal treaties and, unlike NATO, each is on a bilateral basis. There are both benefits and liabilities to this one-on-one arrangement. Life is much simpler and, therefore, more efficient than is found in NATO, where coordination involves 16 nations instead of two. In the Pacific you can strike a deal with your ally and then implement.

The flip side is the absence of centralized command and control for military operations within the region. Regional coordination is on an ad hoc basis and is normally performed by U.S. Commander in Chief, Pacific Command (USCINCPAC).The arrangement suggests a great deficiency, but, in reality, it works about as well as NATO does in Europe.

As for nonallied friends, each is addressed on a bilateral basis with the objective of establishing a close, mutually supportive relationship. USCINCPAC has developed a concept called the "peacetime strategy" to achieve this objective. The idea is to use capabilities inherent in military organizations to cement relations with friendly countries. Activities range from humanitarian assistance to exchange programs to full blown combined military exercises. The concept has worked especially well in the South Pacific, where the U.S. image was suffering from 40 years of neglect and abuse. Thanks to the work of the State Department and the military, that image is changing.

The United States is seen in the Pacific as slipping in an economic sense, but there are no questions about our military might. One-half of the U.S. Navy, two-thirds of the fighting Marines, three Army divisions, and three numbered Air Forces impress friend and foe alike. Unlike Europe, U.S. military forces in the Pacific are regarded as superior to Soviet forces, mostly because of the fighting capabilities of the U.S. Navy. In recent years, the Soviets have added "state-of-the-art" submarines, destroyers, cruisers, aircraft, and artillery to their Pacific forces, but they remain outgunned and outclassed by the U.S. Navy. The high quality found in all our forces, combined with the good health of the network of alliances and friendships, make for restful sleep among those who have responsibility for Pacific Basin security. The occasional nightmare is about future funding support and policy shifts out of Washington, not about today's security posture.

The most important of the mutual security treaties is also the most controversial. Many voices in our democracy have become strident about our partnership with Japan. Several expressions have become commonplace: "Japan is getting a free ride;" "Japan must spend more on defense, but she must not remilitarize;" "Japan has used funds which should have gone into defense to beat us at the marketplace;" "Japan is succeeding economically in Hawaii where in earlier times she failed militarily."

In all the examples cited, economics, not military or political frictions, are the root of the complaint.

If asked 20 years ago what we hoped to see in the future of Japan we would likely have said a democratic society, a sound economy, and a solid security relationship. Today, we see all three in full bloom and don't seem to know how to handle it.

With so much negative publicity, it may be useful to review the bidding. Japan did restrict herself to 1 percent of gross national product for self defense between 1976 and 1987. The reasons for this limit can be found in the strong antimilitary sentiment, actively encouraged by the United States, that developed after World War II among the Japanese people. In addition to the genuine antimilitary feelings, the Japanese people also are well aware that all of Asia would become alarmed if a large military build-up occurred. Memories of World War II still are strong throughout Asia.

Another justification for such a small financial commitment to defense was the reliance on U.S. military forces in the country and the guarantees of the mutual defense treaty. The U.S. guarantees are important because the Japanese are worried about the Soviets, far more so than most Americans, and as long as the Soviets occupy the Japanese Northern Territories, the worry will persist.

What is not generally appreciated by the American people is the impact of a sustained 1 percent investment with a rapidly expanding economy. The year-to-year rate of growth of the Japanese defense budget has been the highest in the world; it today stands as the third largest, although well behind the Soviet Union and the United States. To illustrate the dynamics, in 1987, Prime Minister Nakasone convinced the Diet that the 1 percent restriction was ar-

■ *A Soviet IL-38 reconnaissance aircraft is welcomed by an A-6E Intruder and an F/A-18 Hornet to what naval personnel jokingly refer to as NAS, NAS (Naval Air Station, North Arabian Sea). Both aircraft were attached to CVW-5 aboard the aircraft carrier MIDWAY (CV-41), which was deployed in the Indian Ocean when this encounter took place last September.*

bitrary and should be eliminated in favor of full funding of the Diet-approved mid-term defense plan. The change, also actively encouraged by the United States, was a major policy shift that would allow military needs rather than a fixed amount to be the focus in the planning process. With this new freedom, the mid-term defense plan was fully funded, but an unanticipated spurt in the economy still caused the 1987 defense budget to come in under 1 percent.

It may have been only 1 percent, but the results are impressive. The military hardware is defensively oriented, "state-of-the-art," well maintained, and increasingly of indigenous origin. The forces are well led, well trained, and well disciplined. Defensive strategies are valid, including the responsibility to defend its sea approaches out 1,000 miles.

Efforts are underway to develop the next five-year defense plan and, unlike our own five-year defense plan, which is more wishful thinking than fact, the Japanese plan will become reality, if past practice is continued. The planning dialogue is spirited, and as an indication of just how far Japan has come militarily, such things as nuclear submarines, aircraft carriers (small defensive ones to be sure), airborne tankers, and long-range strike aircraft are under consideration. The real question is not whether Japan can afford these weapon systems, but whether the people of Japan and the countries of Asia will tolerate them.

Today Japan is the world's second leading economic power—some say the first—with extensive investments in research and development, expanding overseas assistance programs, and impressive military forces. As a team, the United States and Japan can cover all aspects of security in Northeast Asia from nuclear deterrence to day-to-day posturing. We have

many goals and aspirations in common, and the military-to-military relationship is as good as the economic relationship is bad. To concentrate on the negative in an era of growing competition around the world is self-denial of opportunity needed for our own competitiveness. Furthermore, if unrestrained conflict and confrontation were to develop as a result of economics, the consequences would be catastrophic for everyone. As military partners, we make a formidable team; economically, there is work to be done.

The second treaty in Northeast Asia is unique, because it is the result of a war that has never ended officially. The Korean conflict continues, and if there are disbelievers, a trip to the demilitarized zone (DMZ) between North and South Korea will convince otherwise. One finds a high degree of military alert, and soldiers on both sides postured to engage rapidly and fiercely.

The passage of time since the cease-fire agreement was signed 37 years ago has not been kind to the North Koreans. Under the inflexible communist regime of Kim Il Sung, revered as a god by most North Koreans, the economy is a basket case, the technological age is nowhere in sight, personal freedoms are denied, and the standard of living is abysmal. Twenty-five percent of the gross national product goes toward support of a 850,000-man army—a guarantee for continuing economic destitution.

Most believe there will be major turmoil with the passing of the elder Kim, now in his late seventies. The first dynastic succession in a communist country to the less competent son is not likely to succeed for long but, with or without the son's success, it would be folly to assume that the North Koreans soon will become our friends.

On the other hand, in the south of the peninsula, one finds a vibrant economy, developing democratic processes, and a respectable standard of living. Growth in the economy has been in the double digit category, personal freedoms have increased, and military capabilities, financed by about the same 6 percent of gross national product as our own, have improved markedly. As a reflection of growing national self-confidence, South Korea has embarked on a new "Northern Policy" to establish diplomatic and trading relationships with socialist countries.

With this remarkable success there comes, quite correctly, the inevitable reevaluation of the merits of the treaty with the United States. It is widely accepted that the United States has been the major factor in maintaining peace on the peninsula for an extended period and that the United States has contributed to the economic success now enjoyed. The Korean leadership heartedly endorses the United States presence as vital for continuing security, yet the "man of the street," who most likely was born after the Korean conflict, questions the need for the prominent U.S. presence.

The U.S. presence consists of the 42nd Army Infantry division, the Seventh Air Force, and a small U.S. Navy mission. The U.S. forces occupy valuable real estate; they have a high profile in Korean society, and impact the traditional culture. Each U.S. military person present costs Korea about $50,000. The Combined Forces Command (CFC), consisting of 43,000 Americans and 600,000 Koreans, makes up the finest combined force in the world today. The force trains together, uses common procedures, has interoperable equipment, and is led by an integrated staff commanded by an American four-star general. If called upon to defend South Korea, the CFC will do well in combat. The question in the minds of South Koreans is not whether the Combined Forces Command will be successful in defending the country, but why South Korean forces are commanded by an American general.

With steadily expanding military capabilities in the South Korean forces and economic stagnation in the north, the time is approaching when South Korea will be able to defend itself. The question being asked with increasing frequency in Washington as well as in Seoul is "When?" The answer depends on the imponderables of political and military affairs. It may well be today or five years hence, but in deliberating such matters, it should be remembered that history favors those who take the cautious route. Furthermore, the deliberations thus far about force withdrawal have been inadequate because the impact on regional security, as opposed to peninsula security, has not been a part of the dialogue. The Koreans traditionally focus only on the peninsula and discount security matters elsewhere as none of their business. With Korea's thrust towards big-power status and her "Northern Policy" with socialist countries, Korean interest in regional security matters will grow. In the United States, the urge is to pull out and avoid costs to support an ally now capable of defending herself. Such an attitude, even where valid, fails to consider our fundamental strategy of forward defense. Quite aside from the defense of the peninsula, forces in Korea, while not optimally tailored for regional operations, are an important part of the forward defense strategy that provides regional stability and keeps the Soviets off our shores.

Japan and Korea are the nexus of U.S. security interest in northeast Asia, the most important region in the Pacific. In northeast Asia two communist giants are undergoing great change and considerable turmoil. Only a few years ago, the People's Republic of China (PRC), with its movement towards free enterprise and more openness, seemed the more promising of the two. Today, the Soviet Union, with *perestroika* and *glasnost*, is on top. The reversal can serve as a sobering reminder of the uncertainties in the world today, the speed with which things can change in a totalitarian society, and the need to avoid precipitous change in our own security posture. Af-

The Problem of Distances
(in miles)

United States to Persian Gulf by shortest air route:	
from East Coast	7,450
from West Coast	8,150
Charleston, S.C., to Strait of Hormuz:	
through Suez	8,250
around Africa	11,500
San Diego to Strait of Hormuz	11,477
to Singapore	7,736
to Manila	6,604
to Sydney	6,530
Lajes Field (Azores):	
to Cairo	3,155
to Dhahran	4,325
Torrejon Air Force Base (Spain) to Cairo	1,960
Aswan (Egypt) to Strait of Hormuz	1,304
Berbera (Somalia) to Strait of Hormuz	1,350
Mombasa (Kenya) to Strait of Hormuz	2,500
Diego Garcia:	
to Dhahran	2,600
to Strait of Hormuz	2,500
to Tehran	2,959
to Freemantle (Australia)	2,850
to Singapore	2,227
to Clark Field (Philippines)	3,445
Singapore:	
to Honolulu	5,881
to Al Basrah (Iraq)	3,916
to Port Said	5,018
Cape of Good Hope:	
to New York	6,801
to Sundra Strait	5,164
to Straits of Florida	6,784

Source: Distances from Ports, Defense Mapping Agency

ter hundreds of exchange visits, technically advanced assistance programs, $14 billion annually in trade, thousands of "gambais" to eternal friendship, and repeated assurances by China's top leaders that there would never be a return to the "old ways," the "old ways" returned over the course of a single evening. We rushed in during the thaw with our technology, dollars, and friendship because of an honest desire to help a nation moving towards more freedom for its people and because of a belief that we could use the friendly relationship to counter the Soviets in the Pacific. Neither motive was flawed because, at the time, there was genuine movement towards free enterprise, and China had more problems and more dislike for the Soviets than we had. Nevertheless, the widely held beliefs that the costs of a return to hardline policies would be too high for the Chinese leadership to pay and that the leadership was increasingly sensitive to world public opinion were testimonials to American gullibility.

Militarily, the traditional focus of China has been land power, pointed to the north along the common border with the Soviet Union. In recent years, the Chinese Navy has gotten more attention because of concerns about a rapidly growing Soviet Pacific Navy and encirclement by the Soviet Union. In a page from Mahan, the Chinese Navy also got a boost from the

ALLISON MARINE ENGINES HAVE BEEN PROVEN ONLY IN THE AREAS CAREFULLY MARKED IN BLUE.

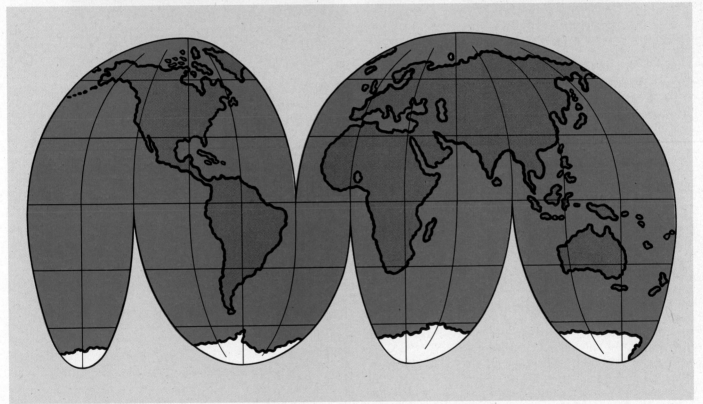

Since 1962, Allison engines have been called on for maritime propulsion and to create on-board electrical power in every corner of the globe.

The reason for all this is simple. We build reliability into each engine we make. Reliability that's been proven in harsh environments in the air, on land, and on the deepest, most hostile saltwater seas.

Allison engines have over 3,000,000 hours of cumulative maritime operating experience and over 100,000,000 hours of aviation and industrial experience. Our engines also have high maintainability plus worldwide support from our extensive parts and service network.

In addition, Allison is General Motors. So, the expertise of the world's largest engineering and manufacturing company is behind each engine.

Write to Allison Gas Turbine, General Motors Corporation, P.O. Box 420, U-6, Indianapolis, Indiana 46206 USA. Telex 6876054.

Allison

© 1987 Allison Gas Turbine

belief that a measure of a nation's international status was naval strength. No doubt this thought was behind the Chinese Navy ship visit to Honolulu in April, the first ever to a U.S. port.

Antiquated equipment plagues the Chinese Air Force, a serious problem that is common to all her services. The need to modernize across the board was widely recognized and plans to do so, with U.S. help, were in place. Since resources were very limited, funds for military upgrade were to come from a 25 percent reduction in end strength, from four million to three million men, and from profits from the export of military hardware. Interestingly, it was President Yang Shang Kun, the individual who directed the People's Liberation Army in quelling the students in Tiananmen Square, who briefed USCINCPAC in Honolulu on the details of the plan to reduce the size of the Army by one million men. Today, no such discussion would occur.

The Tiananmen Square massacre brings into question the legitimacy of the Communist Party and its prospects for retaining power. No group seems adequately organized to contest the rule of the party, but with the widespread malaise that has settled in and the advanced ages of key leaders, the future holds both instability and unpredictability.

Whether hard-line communism or something more palatable emerges in Beijing, China, by its very size and population, is a force to reckon with in the Pacific. More than a billion *plus* hard working people, many of whom yearn for opportunity and freedom, cannot be ignored or taken for granted. The Chinese attitude is, if not today, then next week or next year or perhaps within the next 50 to 100 years. In our dealings with China, we would benefit from the same perspective and accept that a pluralist democracy and a market-oriented economy is in the making, but years may pass before it happens.

Off the Chinese east coast, within artillery range of the mainland, is the island of Kinmen, which is claimed by Taiwan. Most Americans would recognize the island by the name "Quemoy." Fierce fighting took place there in 1949 and again in 1958, when Communist China attempted to take Quemoy and her sister islands by force. Devastation was widespread, but Chiang Kai-shek's determined defenders hung on, and the free world declared a great victory over the evil forces of communism. The struggling "Republic of China," with material assistance from the United States, had denied the communists' major objective to place Taiwan behind the "bamboo curtain." Today, Kinmen is a showplace with trees, green grass, productive farms, thriving entrepreneurs, and friendly people. Kinmen is not unlike Taiwan as a whole. It stands in marked contrast to conditions on the mainland.

Most nations, including the United States and Taiwan, agree that there is only one China, but two "systems." The system in Taiwan has produced an incredi-

■ *A Thai woman talks to a Marine as he paints his face before entering the jungle during exercise Thalay Thai.*

ble country where progress is the most important product. Militarily, there is a force to be reckoned with. People in uniform are well trained, serious minded, and dedicated professionals. An equipment modernization program is underway; the military are developing their own next generation fighter aircraft and embarking on a major frigate program for the Navy. We have no formal diplomatic relations with the country, since the ''One China'' we recognize is located in Beijing. We do not even use the title ''Republic of China'' in official correspondence for fear of offending the People's Republic. Neither do we have direct military-to-miliary ties beyond the sale of military hardware. There are no Navy port visits, exchange programs, or bilateral exercises.

Despite the prohibitions on diplomatic and military activities, commerce between the two countries is thriving, and we are good friends who would be mutually supportive in times of crises or conflict.

Several hundred miles south of Taiwan lies a struggling nation of 7,000 islands, racked by a communist insurgency, but blessed by likeable people and abundant natural resources. The Republic of the Philippines is formally allied with the United States through a mutual defense treaty. Strategically important U.S. bases at Subic Bay and Clark Air Base are authorized through the treaty. For this reason, this treaty also has become controversial. Many Philippine leaders believe that the treaty with its associated bases infringes on sovereign rights, and one hears the claim that the treaty, and therefore the bases, are for our benefit, not that of the Philippines, which has no external enemies. Some of this thinking can be charged to the desire to extract as much from the United States for a new base agreement, needed by 1991, as the traffic will bear. From a negotiating position, there is nothing wrong with a strategy to make the best deal, but in the process there is the risk of aggravating the love-hate relationship between the two countries that has existed since Admiral Dewey arrived in Manila Bay with his battle fleet at the turn of the century. Today, a consensus favors continuation of the treaty relationship and its associated base structure, but key leaders say otherwise. The underlying politics are complex, and, for the most part, unfathomable for most non-Filipinos.

The survival of democracy in the Philippines no longer seems to be in question. Democratic institutions are in place to deal with the root causes of the insurgency, the armed forces have shifted their focus to military operations even though there is a restive element that breaks out from time to time, and the economic decline has been reversed. By no means, however, is Manila out of the woods. Passage through Ninoy Aquino International Airport brings the point home. Immigration and customs functions are handled efficiently and with courtesy, but the sense of orderliness changes abruptly once the front

■ *Marines fight aggressors in a Thai field during exercise Thalay Thai in 1989.*

doors are cleared. The visitor is confronted with underprivileged masses of humanity, most very young, milling around with no apparent purpose. Travel through the crowd to curbside reveals a street overcrowded with vintage automobiles, many of which are belching smoke from the tail pipe. A common sight is an individual with a handkerchief over his face in the futile effort to breathe clean air.

The scene illustrates a fundamental problem in the Philippines today—an out-of-control population growth that checkmates the positive role of growth in the economy. The standard of living ought to be improving with the quickening pace of business activity, but the street people and the cardboard shacks along Roxos Boulevard are as numerous today as they were during the Marcos regime.

Despite these conditions, there is hope for the future and a willingness by donor nations to provide financial support. Relations with the United States will remain contentious, but not so contentious as to prevent a new agreement on base access. If, by an unfortunate turn, agreement is not realized, there are alternatives to the Philippine bases that are workable, but not nearly as suitable.

The Republic of the Philippines is the least prosperous of the six members of the Association of South East Asia Nations (ASEAN), an organization founded in 1967 for the purpose of consultation in political matters. Other members are Indonesia, Malaysia, Singapore, Brunei, and ally Thailand. No economic or military dimension was initially intended. Success of the organization has surprised many who believed member nations' interests were too diverse and too parochial for effective coordination. ASEAN's role in Cambodia's occupation by Vietnam is a case in point. The Vietnamese easily won a military victory, but ASEAN's solidarity prevented a political victory.

With progress in consultation and cooperation on the political side realized, it is logical to assume that in future years ASEAN will collaborate on economic and military matters as well. Already, the military chiefs meet from time to time and the need for intra-ASEAN economic cooperation is evident among the member nations. In fact, it is generally believed that economic cooperation among themselves and with other Pacific countries will displace the Cambodian occupation as the matter of greatest importance to ASEAN.

After ten years of war in Cambodia, the Vietnamese have pulled out, and efforts are underway to form a new government. The resolute stand taken by the ASEAN nations is partly responsible for the withdrawal. Stubborn resistance by displaced Cambodians who took up arms and a collapsed economy in Vietnam are other reasons the campaign failed. Despite this favorable development, it is premature to claim victory. The Khmer Rouge, who massacred over a million of their countrymen in the late 1970s and caused the Vietnamese invasion in the first place, remain the best organized and best equipped element of the resistance forces. These PRC-supported communists could quickly fill any vacuum caused by the Vietnamese departure and could cause yet another era of darkness for the Cambodian people.

ASEAN's front-line state in the conflict has been Thailand, a good friend and ally of the United States. Thailand has borne the brunt of the refugee problem, has seen repeated military incursions across her sovereign border, and has suffered thousands of personnel casualties. Despite such problems, the attitude of Thailand has been resolute, and, faced with adversity, the relationship between the United States and Thailand has improved. In recent years, on the military side, personnel exchange programs, hardware programs, and combined exercises have expanded in ways that serve mutual interest and contribute to regional security. For example, the bilateral agreement to preposition U.S. war reserve ammunition in Thailand is a strong signal of commitment that has not been missed in Indo-China.

A less volatile region is Oceania in the South Pacific, although the image of carefree people in a tropical paradise represents a bygone era. A military coup in Fiji, political violence in Vanuatu and New Caledonia, civil strife in Papua New Guinea, meddling by outsiders, including Libyans, and struggling economics clash with the tranquil stereotype. Attention and support are needed from the developed countries—and a willingness to bring the Islanders along at the pace they, not others, believe is correct.

A continuing problem in the South Pacific for our deterrence strategy is the pervasive antinuclear sentiment that has developed from past use of the region for nuclear-weapons tests. Tests by the French still are occurring in French Polynesia. Anxiety also is fostered by the persistent rumor that developed countries intend to dump chemical and nuclear waste in what outsiders consider to be the vast area of unused, unwanted, and useless ocean of the South Pacific.

With an abiding concern about the impact of nuclear operations on the environment in the South Pacific, logic that supports a nuclear deterrent posture falls on deaf ears. Already antinuclear sentiments have caused New Zealand to drop out of the Australia-New Zealand-United States (ANZUS) treaty, and despite a recent change in government, there are no indications of a reversal. The impact is strained relations between two old friends and former allies and less security for New Zealand and the Pacific at large.

Some compensation for the loss of New Zealand has been realized by a more meaningful and much stronger military relationship with Australia. Military-to-military activity has expanded, and combined exercises are more frequent and of higher quality. Under the capable leadership of Prime Minister Robert Hawke and his Minister of Defense, Kim Beasley, an extensive review of security policy appropriate to Australia has been completed with results that

■ *Chinese naval personnel man the rail of the visiting training ship* Zheng He *as she is escorted to her berth in Pearl Harbor by the large harbor tug* Neodosha *(YTB-815). This visit last April was the first ever by a ship of the navy of the People's Republic of China. Commissioned in 1987, she is the only new Chinese Navy training ship.*

received widespread acclaim and acceptance. Australia always has been a valued ally, and there is no reason to believe the future will see otherwise.

Our Pacific alliances serve us well, but alliances are best when the danger is most evident. The evident danger has been the expanding warfighting capability of the Soviet Union east of the Urals. Force structure numbers have increased prominently, but the greatest concerns for defense planners have been caused by the increasing modernity of the Soviet military machine. With the introduction of Backfire, Badger, and Fencer aircraft equipped with cruise missiles, increasingly quiet submarines, modern warships, and mobility and firepower systems for land forces, the ability to engage in offensive operations is convincing.

Today, the danger is less evident. Pacific leaders are being hosted in Moscow, diplomatically the Soviets are scoring throughout the region, Vladivostok has been declared an "open city," there is talk about the Soviet Navy visiting San Diego, and the long-standing dispute between the Soviet Union and the People's Republic of China is receding. Soviet troop reductions actually are occurring in Asia as pledged by President Gorbachev last December. In a recent announcement, Gorbachev stated that 12 army divisions, 11 air regiments, and 16 warships in the Pacific would be demobilized.

Such developments are indeed encouraging, but the troop cuts are being made in border garrisons facing China, with little change in the line-up against U.S. and Japanese forces. Furthermore, the qualitative improvements that cause the greatest concern have not changed. Evidence of the much-talked-about defensive shift in Soviet military doctrine is not apparent in the Pacific.

We face the challenge of change and 45 years of successful economic and political restructuring. During the period we have conducted surgical strikes, most of which turned out messily, suffered terrorist attacks, provided protective service for nations around the globe, fought limited wars, and engaged in continuous cold war. Our batting average is not too bad. Democracy and free enterprise are in vogue, and the cold war, while it might be premature to declare victory, seems less relevant with each pronouncement from the Kremlin.

In a security sense, our military forces are as capable as they have ever been in peacetime, our alliance network is in good health, and our principal adversary, the Soviet Union, seems less and less threatening.

Today the challenge is the inevitable paradox that accompanies success. The feeling of security gives rise to complacency and unwillingness to make the continuing sacrifices necessary to maintain the conditions that led to success. The Soviets are as aware of this truism as we are, but at this point, it is we, not they, who have to worry about the paradox of success.

Clearly, change is occurring in the Soviet Union, and we have been heartened by what we have seen and heard. *Glasnost* and *perestroika* are concepts that Westerners can identify with and endorse; they also are concepts designed to save a faltering nation, not to change a foreign policy that embraces a Socialist world under the leadership of the Soviet Union. The facts seem to support that classic communist ideology and centrally controlled economy are abysmal failures, but to believe that the competition for the hearts and minds of men in this new era will fade away is wishful thinking.

What extraordinary times! We are living in a more prosperous and safer world that has not seen major war in 45 years. In our pride of accomplishment, we would do well to remember that a convincing deterrent posture based on well-trained, capable, and ready military forces and alliance solidarity has gotten us to where we are today. Our game plan of peace through military strength has worked, and it will be peace through military strength that will take us successfully into the next century.

Force Reductions Won't Diminish NATO Need for Reliable Merchant Shipping

These are times of great change in the making of the tapestry of international and inter-alliance relations. For 40 years, NATO has devoted its efforts to readiness and plans to counter the Soviet threat. That threat has been characterized by images of Ivan the Terrible or his latter-day look alikes. Today we are inundated with a "new, improved" Soviet Union as proclaimed by "Gorbachev the Bearable." As the infatuation of the Western world with Gorbachev grows, talk of arms control and major U.S. force reductions in Europe have become the topic of conversations in government halls and family homes alike.

Glasnost and *perestroika* may be harbingers of what one scholar terms the "post-post-war era," but we must be realistic. Although accommodation may be possible in East-West relations, great caution is still required. History repeatedly has demonstrated the inherent incompatability between the principles of democracy and the doctrine of communism. While the Soviets may be sincere in their desire for a stable and peaceful common European home, they are unlikely to negotiate away the only foundation of their superpower status—military might.

By ISAAC C. KIDD

ADMIRAL ISAAC C. KIDD retired in 1978 after serving for three years as Supreme Allied Commander, Atlantic, and Commander, U.S. Forces, Atlantic. During his 40-year career, which included 28 years in sea assignments, he was heavily involved in maritime logistics, including naval procurement, and planning for and meeting short- and long-range air- and sea-lift requirements. Since retirement he has served as an advisor to NATO, the Defense and State Departments, the General Accounting Office, and the Congress, and as a member of the Defense Science Board.

Bound together by a common pledge, the North Atlantic Treaty signatories have, for four decades, resolved to maintain a free and democratic Europe. This 40-year commitment, backed by a combined military capability, is based on Alliance cohesion, political will, and a clear understanding of what is in the collective best interest of the Alliance. NATO's continued success can only be assured if we enter this "post-post-war era" with a practical and reasonable strategy that maintains, as a minimum, and enhances, where possible, our collective position as an Alliance. I am particularly concerned that flexibility inherent in overall seapower, sealift, and shipping policies which remain the major building block of this strategy not be overlooked or subordinated in our haste to embrace the Soviet Bear. We have yet to see his entire hand. It is my bet that among his unplayed cards is the demand for savage cuts in what we have that he envys most—men of war and that for which they exist, i.e., merchant fleets. Best we be prepared.

Regardless of the outcome of present or future East-West negotiations, the role of NATO's military force and merchant shipping fleets remains unchanged. We must maintain a credible defense capability to deter the enemy from aggression and, if deterrence fails, we must be able to act decisively to protect the interest of the Alliance members. To those of us on the North American shores of the Atlantic, this means possessing a credible continuing capability to reinforce and resupply Europe as a deterrent in crisis or to win a war. Transportation of large numbers of personnel and equipment across an ocean is not an insignificant task. This mission, originally conceived as the Iron Curtain descended over Europe, is really a three-part operation, each important to the survival of the Alliance:

1. Reinforcement and resupply of North American forces committed to the conflict. This includes some 8.5 million tons of dry cargo and 15 million tons of petroleum, oil, and lubricants (POL) in the first 180 days of fighting.

2. Resupply of European NATO military forces. This requirement is estimated at 7.2 million tons of dry cargo and 9.6 million tons of POL in the first 180 days.

3. Economic shipping for NATO economies, largely composed of essential raw materials required to sustain industrial production and the civilian populations of the Alliance. Economic shipping for North America totals over 365 million tons annually. NATO

European imports are estimated at more than 945 million tons annually. To maintain even 70 percent of this trade would require sufficient ships to move almost 76 million tons of cargo a month.

Although all three components of the reinforcement mission are important, I wish to focus attention on the military reinforcement and resupply of Europe for one major reason. In the anticipation of "bringing the boys home" now, some people have lost sight of an important fact, namely, conventional forces in a post-INF Europe will assume an increased importance. Furthermore, conventional-force reductions will make the Alliance's dependence on North America reinforcements and resupply efforts even greater than they are now. In my mind, current discussions should serve to underscore the critical requirement for control of the Atlantic sea lanes and underline our continued reliance on merchant shipping.

Arms control measures that maintain or improve the stability we have enjoyed since the end of World War II are to be welcomed and applauded. While we do not yet know the ultimate outcome of the current deliberations, wide-ranging changes are inevitable. My purpose in this essay is to discuss arms control in the context of sealift and to highlight some of the complexities that may be created by these changes. Admiral Frank B. Kelso II, NATO's Supreme Allied Commander Atlantic (SACLANT), gives this assessment of the situation: "With the prospect of reduced troop and equipment levels in Europe, our ability to ensure the uninterrupted flow of men, weapons, oil, raw materials, and trade across the Atlantic and around the world takes on added significance."

Depending upon the reductions, SACLANT's job of keeping the sea lanes open may be less a daunting task as a result of arms control or force reductions. However, it is my view that these negotiations do not diminish our vulnerability as an Alliance dependent on the sea bridge to Europe, nor do they decrease NATO's requirement for reliable merchant shipping. On the contrary, recent events serve to illustrate our growing dependence on the sea lanes and on merchant shipping.

At the NATO ministers' meeting held 29 May 1989 at the North Atlantic Treaty Organization headquarters in Brussels, President Bush ushered in NATO's fifth decade with a bold offer to remove 30,000 American troops from Europe in exchange for a Soviet reduction of 300,000 troops. This asymmetrical force reduction is intended to bring about a balance of force in Europe. Earlier this year, Gorbachev offered to reduce the Soviet military by 500,000 troops. In addition to these presidential exchanges conducted through the public air waves, more traditional negotiating teams from the NATO and Warsaw Pact nations are engaged in discussions that undoubtedly will influence the nature and quantity of armed forces in Europe. In contrast to the old

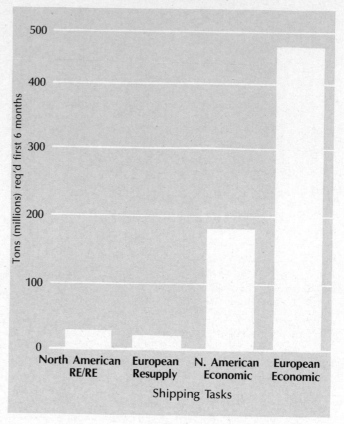

Alliance Shipping Requirements
(in time of crisis or war)

Tons (millions) req'd first 6 months

Shipping Tasks: North American RE/RE, European Resupply, N. American Economic, European Economic

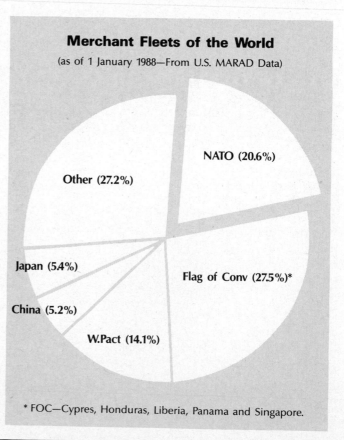

Merchant Fleets of the World
(as of 1 January 1988—From U.S. MARAD Data)

NATO (20.6%)
Other (27.2%)
Flag of Conv (27.5%)*
Japan (5.4%)
China (5.2%)
W.Pact (14.1%)

* FOC—Cypres, Honduras, Liberia, Panama and Singapore.

Mutual and Balanced Force Reduction negotiations (MBFR), which covered only Central Europe, the nations represented at the new Conventional Forces in Europe (CFE) talks are discussing ways and means of reducing the number of armed forces and non-nuclear weapons across Europe from the Atlantic to the Urals (ATTU). These negotiations, initiated 9 March 1989, will, if successful, have a significant impact on current military plans and operations.

This most important decision of how large or small a standing force to retain in Europe is, of course, a political one to be resolved both within and between alliances. That is not an easy task, judging from the 15 years of stalled MBFR talks abandoned earlier this year in Vienna. The focus has shifted from manpower to equipment, but even when there is agreement in principle to include an item for discussion, there is considerable wrangling over definition and identification of items such as main battle tanks. By some estimates, as many as 100,000 major pieces of military equipment are to be identified, destroyed, and verified under the current Atlantic-to-the-Urals negotiations. The equipment identified in the proposal advanced by President Bush in May for the withdrawal and demobilization of 30,000 U.S. troops—tanks, armored troop carriers, artillery pieces, and land-based planes and helicopters—is to be withdrawn and destroyed.

While the ultimate outcome of these East-West discussions remains an open question, at this point it would appear that there could be some reduction in the size of NATO forces currently stationed in Europe, perhaps even beyond those recently proposed by President Bush. The magnitude and composition of the conventional force reductions, whether all affected NATO personnel are retained on active duty, placed in reserve, or demobilized, are entirely undecided. Will withdrawn equipment be left in designated European depots, or will it come home with returning troops to be placed in national storage sites, or are we really going to beat our swords into plowshares? What military strength do we deem adequate to deter aggression and then to protect the vital interests of individual nations and the Alliance as a whole?

From a military perspective, strength determination is a statement of the acceptable or desirable force-balance ratio—the ratio of NATO forces to Warsaw Pact forces. "Force" must be defined rather clearly—not an easy thing to do. It may couched in terms of combat capability; numbers of combat soldiers, airmen, and sailors; or some olive-drab blend of tanks, artillery, and bombs. For our purpose we will consider the force balance ratio (FBR) to be the ratio of land-based uniformed soldiers in each of the two Alliances. This scale is used because it is the equipment of those uniformed personnel that must be considered in the sealift problem, and because it allows certain generalizations appropriate for this discussion.*

Expert opinions of an acceptable FBR to defend NATO's position range from as lean as 2:1 in favor of the Warsaw Pact to as ample as 1.2:1 in favor of the Warsaw Pact.[1] While these figures refer to FBRs in time of war, the credibility of an in-place active force deterrent may be thought of in roughly the same terms. The current FBR of about 1.4:1 (3,090,000 Warsaw Pact to 2,213,593 NATO) in favor of the Warsaw Pact[2] is within the range suggested by William P. Mako.**

The 30,000 troop reduction proposed by President Bush does not significantly change the present FBR. A 500,000 troop reduction by the Soviet Union, on the other hand, would reduce the Warsaw Pact advantage to approximately 1.2:1. The final negotiated range is likely somewhere in the middle of these figures, though "a radical restructuring of the forces of NATO and the Warsaw Pact, on the basis of parity, with total active forces on each side at no more than 50 percent of present NATO strength,"[3] as proposed by a former Supreme Allied Commander, Europe, and retired U.S. Army General, Andrew J. Goodpaster, should not necessarily be discounted.

Decisions affecting North American forces are of special concern, given their reliance on the ocean routes for transporting reinforcement and resupply equipment. At present the United States and Canada maintain 10 percent of the ground forces currently in Europe.[4] American and Canadian forces combined also represent about 40 percent of the total of military forces maintained by NATO nations. These two measurements, 10 and 40 percent, could be construed as plausible lower and upper limits to guide discussions surrounding removal of North American troops from Europe.

The final disposition of the North American forces removed from Europe is especially important to consider. Will the troops come home and remain active within the confines of their own country, will they be placed in reserve, or will they be totally disbanded? The answers to these questions directly determine the extent and speed with which they could be reconstituted and redeployed in the event of crisis or war. They are, of course, in addition to the approximately 1.5 million other North American personnel already planned for the reinforcement of Europe. Unlike our European allies who do not rely on sea lanes to reach the battlefield, we must consider the fate of equipment withdrawn to North America which has a direct impact on reinforcement shipping requirements. We must be concerned about the final disposition of all drawn-down forces, since over 90 percent of the equipment required by North American reinforcements is totally dependent on sealift to deliver it to Europe.

Balanced force reductions are of particular importance to our Alliance, which is both divided and drawn together by a vast ocean. Force reductions may be popularly supported and almost irresistible, but we must proceed with caution. A decision to remove military equipment from Europe may resolve a short-term political question but intensify long-term strategic defense issues for the Alliance.

The destruction of all withdrawn equipment and the associated lost operational ability would, of course, be of prime concern to NATO's military planners. One could anticipate that the sight of operational equipment being burned or crushed also might cause taxpayers and budget committee members in Congress some anxiety. Removal and storage of equipment is an alternative, but this, too, presents certain problems. Stored equipment is of no value unless it is maintained in a state affording easy access and assured reliability. Such a program would entail significant costs. Taking it home to be carted back to the theater of operation presents a bigger problem, particularly for those forces that must be lifted across the North Atlantic. Adding to our sealift problem does not enhance NATO's credibility or operational effectiveness.

Consideration of the number of North Americans identified to reinforce Europe in the event of crisis or war cannot be isolated from the arms control process. If major force reductions in the ATTU are realized, along the lines of those proposed by President Bush or suggested by Goodpaster, we could expect as a consequence that the acceptable FBR may be achieved with fewer U.S. and Canadian reinforcements.

Under current plans, the United States and Canada have promised to reinforce NATO Europe with nearly 1.5 million additional personnel. Not all of these are ground force combatants. Some are support or staff personnel, seamen, and airmen. Each of them, however, requires certain equipment to perform his mission.

Some of the equipment intended for use by North American reinforcements already is in Europe, in storage, under a program called POMCUS (Prepositioning of Material Configured in Unit Sets). POMCUS represents but a small proportion of the required equipment, about 15 percent. Decisions made as a part of the arms-control process may change the amount of equipment stored in Europe. It is possible that some U.S. or Canadian combat personnel will be brought home and their gear left in place. Such a move would be roughly analogous to a Soviet withdrawal of troops and equipment to a location east of the Ural mountains; ready for rapid redeployment to the ATTU, adding a little time to the "rising tensions" phase of an impending conflict, but no real force reduction would have occurred. If, on the other hand, equipment is removed to North America and maintained ready for redeployment, it could not be brought back into play quickly; perhaps several weeks would be required for it to be repositioned in the battlefield. This latter situation has no analogy in the Warsaw Pact. It is the burden of an alliance linked by and dependent on sea lanes of communi-

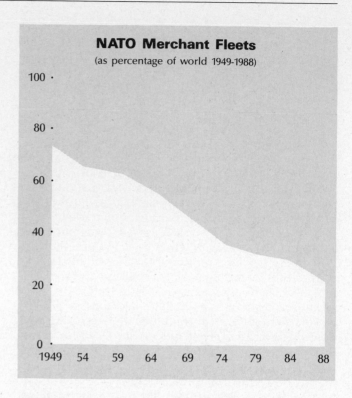

NATO Merchant Fleets
(as percentage of world 1949-1988)

cation that reinforcements cannot be quickly moved forward.

Of the equipment permanently maintained in North America and destined for combat in Europe, over 90 percent must be moved by sea. In a previous essay, I estimated a requirement to sealift some 8.5 million tons of dry cargo and 15 million tons of petroleum, oil, and lubricants (POL) in the first 180 days of fighting, occupying some 1,000 ships.[5] Approximately 900 ships are currently available to move the 8.5 million tons of dry cargo, making the average ship responsible for delivering almost 9,500 tons of weapons, equipment, ammunition, and spare parts safely to Europe.*** In gross terms, then, this means that 8.5 million tons of dry cargo are required to support the nearly 1.5 million reinforcement personnel.**** Recognizing that individual warriors and their associated equipment vary widely, we can generalize and say that, in the aggregate, each person sent in reinforcement represents about 5.6 tons of cargo. Admittedly defining the number of ships required for reinforcement is more complicated than a simple equation of numbers of persons and tons of cargo. It is realistic, however, to anticipate an increased sealift requirement if we add to the number of North American troops to be mobilized for reinforcement. Using the numbers presented above, we can estimate that one ship must provide sealift support for 1,700 persons (1,500,000 men/900 ships). Possible? Wishful thinking.

Is the post-arms-control lift requirement different than the current requirement? The FY 1990 *Annual Report to the Congress* by former Secretary of Defense

Frank C. Carlucci reports that 323,000 U.S. ground and air forces were stationed in Europe at the end of September 1988.[6] President Bush has pressed for U.S. and Soviet troop reductions that would leave each of those two countries with about 275,000 ground and air forces in the ATTU. He further said "all of the reduced equipment would be destroyed."[7] Goodpaster proposes parity "with total active forces on each side no more than 50 percent of present NATO strength."[8] Assuming Goodpaster, like President Bush, also intends for all reduced equipment to be destroyed, the impact on sealift of either of their proposals would be negligible since destroyed equipment needs no sealift. To consider the longer term, the required flow rate of resupply under present plans would be slightly reduced since there would be fewer warriors to support.

On the other hand, if President Bush's offer to destroy reduced equipment is withdrawn and we plan to mobilize and redeploy withdrawn equipment, we have a problem. Under the Bush proposal, we would require approximately 28 additional ships to redeploy unit equipment from North America to Europe. Under the Goodpaster plan, if half the roughly 328,000 North American forces in Europe withdrew with the intent of redeploying at mobilization, we would require approximately 193 additional ships to reinforce Europe—a 48 percent increase over the current stat-

ed requirement. That would put us in dire straits indeed, since we are barely able to meet the current requirement.

At this point, let me say a few words about the third component of reinforcement; namely, the requirement to sustain NATO civilian economies. According to industry sources, world seaborne trade volume increased by 6 percent in 1988 to 3,666 million tons. In the same year, the Organization of Economic Cooperation and Development, comprised primarily of NATO nations, showed a particularly strong growth of 9 percent.[9] There is no reason to believe that the economies of NATO member nations will not continue to show increased growth and demand for marine transportation.

Alliance military requirements for merchant shipping may be significantly affected by the disposition of withdrawn equipment. If equipment is destroyed, requirements are likely to remain constant or decline slightly. This same general conclusion cannot be made regarding requirements to meet civilian needs. Economic shipping requirements will continue to increase as we move into the next century.

I began this essay by asking how initiatives brought about by arms control and force reductions would affect reinforcement sealift. I have attempted to highlight some of the complexities of the issue and to illustrate that ongoing discussions to determine force

■ *If large numbers of Army troops are ordered home from Europe, much of their equipment likely will be transported by this fast sealift ship, the Algol (TAKR-287), and her seven sister ships. These huge 33-knot ships carry large amounts of equipment, but not personnel.*

levels in Europe will have a direct impact on Alliance lift requirements. While the outcome of current discussions remains unclear, it would appear that we could be on the brink of a "brave new world."

Removal of American troops from Europe, as proposed by President Bush, accompanied by the asymmetrical drawdown of Soviet troops, would have a significant impact on NATO's current position in Europe. This should be viewed as a positive first step in promoting peace and stability on a continent that has long known the ravages of war. However, we cannot ignore the consequences of our actions. The most serious impact will be as a result of the decisions regarding the ultimate disposition of withdrawn equipment. If all forces removed are disbanded and associated equipment destroyed, there would likely be no increase in sealift requirements. If, however, the equipment of these withdrawn troops is merely removed from the ATTU region (or destroyed and replaced), we may be faced with a major sealift crisis. Unlike the Soviets, who could swiftly bring their forces and equipment back into play, the success of

NATO's reinforcement plan is dependent on fast sealift. As Secretary General of NATO Manfred Woerner has aptly stated: "Use of the ocean is not an option for NATO; it is a necessity."[10]

We now are just able to meet our stated military sealift requirements. What of the future? Even if we assume that future increases in requirements will be limited to those necessary to sustain economic growth, we cannot ignore an obvious fact: The success of our plan to reinforce and resupply Europe relies on continued access to a shrinking resource—NATO-controlled merchant shipping. Unhappily, in the 12 months since last addressing this subject in the *Almanac of Seapower*, merchant fleets under NATO flags have continued to decline. Successful implementation of current force reduction proposals should provide a short breathing space. We must use that time to reassess the future of NATO shipping and take positive steps to provide the required lift to meet our commitments to the Alliance. The oceans do not negotiate—they never have and never will. They must be dealt with as they are.

(The author wishes to acknowledge the invaluable contributions made by LCdr W. Gregory (USN) and Ms. S. Pond in the preparation of this essay. The able direction of Ralph Nalur in this field continues an international treasure to the alliance.)

*While the overwhelming majority of North American reinforcement personnel will be airlifted to Europe, virtually all of their equipment will be transported by sea.

**In-depth discussions of conventional forces in Europe may be found in *U.S. Ground Forces and the Defense of Central Europe*, by William P. Mako, and in *NATO-WARSAW PACT: Conventional Force Balance: Papers for U.S. and Soviet Perspective Workshops*, Supplement B to a United States General Accounting Office report to the Chairmen, Committees on Armed Services, U.S. Senate and House of Representatives, Washington, D.C., December 1988.

***POL should be treated separately. Its availability and supply to Europe in time of war are subject to influences outside the scope of this discussion. Among them are the size, locations, and availability of product tankers and crude oil carriers, sources of petroleum products, the reserve stores of POL already in Europe and the notion that such products are unlikely to be the subject of arms control agreements.

****Sealifts requirements are, of course, constantly changing. By some reckoning, U.S. Army mechanized divisions are 40 percent heavier today than in 1980. (See B. Schemmer, *Armed Forces Journal International*, May 1989.)

1. William P. Mako, *U.S. Ground Forces and the Defense of Central Europe* (Washington, D.C.: The

Brookings Institution, 1983), p. 38.

2. *Conventional Forces in Europe: THE FACTS*, North Atlantic Treaty Organization (Brussels, November 1988), p. 22. The data, current as of January 1988, "Covers full-time military personnel of Land Forces, including Army personnel who perform ground-based air defense duties. Also included are Command and General Support troops and Other Ministry of Defense troops. Paramilitary forces are excluded."

3. Andrew J. Goodpaster, *Gorbachev and the Future of East-West Security: A Response for the Mid-Term*, an Occasional Paper by The Atlantic Council of the United States (Washington, D.C.: The Atlantic Council of the United States, April 1989) p. 16.

4. *Conventional Forces in Europe: THE FACTS*, op. cit., p. 22.

5. Isaac C. Kidd Jr., "NATO Logistics System Stands in Danger of Collapsing Under Strain of Conflict," in *Almanac of Seapower* (Navy League of the United States, 1989) pp. 62-63.

6. *Report of the Secretary of Defense Frank C. Carlucci to the Congress on the FY 1990/FY 1991 Biennial Budget and FY 1990-94 Defense Programs 17 January 17 1989*.

7. "President's Statement on the New Arms Plan," *New York Times* (29 May 1989).

8. Goodpaster, op. cit., p. 16.

9. Fearnleys, *Review 1988* (Oslo, Norway: Fernresearch, January 1989), p. 4. OECD members are all 16 members of NATO plus Australia, Austria, Finland, Ireland, Japan, New Zealand, Sweden, and Switzerland.

10. Dr. Manfred Woerner, Secretary General of NATO, addressing SEALINK 89 conference, Annapolis, Maryland, 13 June 1989.

Tomorrow's vital defense technologies are sometimes needed sooner than expected.

Only a superior, and sustained, investment in research and development can suffice to meet the challenge of ensuring our future common security. Which is why Aerospatiale stands at the forefront of Europe's aerospace sector as a source of meaningful breakthroughs in defense

aerospatiale

EM02

related technologies. Consider Aster, shown here. When it enters service in the mid-1990's, it will be the only system of its kind in the NATO arsenal capable of effectively stopping saturation attacks by lowflying or diving supersonic missiles. The key to Aster's potency? Our demonstrated lead in such critical areas as miniaturized electronics, advanced propulsion systems, or new in-flight control concepts. Aster, along with systems like Exocet and the nuclear pre-deterrent ASMP, symbolizes our commitment to better defense through better technology. And demonstrates our ability to deliver that technology on-time, on-spec, and consistently in advance of the threat.

DIVISION ENGINS TACTIQUES – 2, RUE BÉRANGER – 92322 CHATILLON CEDEX – FRANCE – TÉL. : (1) 47 46 21 21

Task of Rebuilding Merchant Marine Rests Squarely With President

With the inauguration of George Herbert Walker Bush as the 41st President of the United States in January, the country settled back anticipating few changes in policy from the previous administration. As the year progressed it became increasingly clear that, while this might be the case, the president was firmly committed to his pledge not to increase taxes. Therefore, with few exceptions, any new initiative requiring additional funding was doomed. It is in this environment that the state of the U.S. merchant marine must once again be reviewed.

The year started with the release of the final report of the Commission on Merchant Marine and Defense (the Commission). The report was perhaps as significant for what it chose to ignore as for what it actually presented in its list of recommendations. The Commission, chaired by former Senator Jeremiah Denton, worked long and hard in an effort to determine the current state of the American merchant marine. During a two-year period it also examined existing Defense Department wartime scenarios to relate future logistic requirements to existing and projected U.S. maritime resources. After hearing

By ANDREW E. GIBSON

ANDREW E. GIBSON formerly was president of Delta Steamship lines and for many years a senior executive of Grace Lines. He was Assistant Secretary of Commerce for Maritime Affairs from 1969–1972 and in that capacity developed the Nixon Administration's maritime program and the enabling legislation that became the Merchant Marine Act of 1970. He now holds the Emory S. Land Chair of Maritime Affairs at the Naval War College.

many hours of testimony and accumulating mountains of data, the Commission concluded that "... the deteriorated condition of America's maritime industries presents a clear and growing danger to national security." While its evaluation of the problem was hardly unexpected, the Commission's proposed solutions unfortunately lacked both innovation and political reality.

The Commission had its origins in 1983 when Congressman Charles Bennett (D-FL), chairman of the Seapower Subcommittee of the House Armed Services Committee, held a series of hearings on the subject of military sealift. One result of these hearings was to alert the chairman to the rapid decline of the nation's merchant marine. As a consequence, he determined to create a commission to see what could be done to enable the U.S. shipping industry to carry out its sealift commitments in time of national emergency.

Not long after this effort got underway, the shipbuilders' lobbyists learned of the proposed undertaking and through their several and powerful supporters in the House insisted that the scope of the Commission's work be expanded to include shipbuilding as well. Their successful effort undoubtedly doomed any hope of an objective study that might have identified the real problems affecting the U.S. merchant marine.

The shipbuilders correctly sensed that the need to acquire and repair ships in the world market would be a principal factor in any recommendation aimed at resolving the problems of the American shipowners. They simply were not going to permit this to happen, at least not without extracting a large increase in government funding for themselves.

The shipbuilders were assured that they would be ably represented on the new Commission by having the president of one of the nation's largest shipyards appointed to it. The merchant marine enjoyed no comparable representation since not a single member of the Commission had ever had any executive experience as either a shipowner or an operator. This void undoubtedly contributed to the absence of any indication that increased private investment should be encouraged to participate in bringing about the industry's revitalization. By proposing to leave in place all of the present governmental obstructions in the form of law and regulation, the Commission had no real alternative but to recommend a vast increase in government funding as the solution to the problem it correctly identified. The $13 billion program it put forward was directed primarily at assisting the shipbuilders. It also proposed the adoption of an expansion of various forms of protection for the shipping industry. While such proposals may bring cheers from some of the industry and their congressional allies, they guarantee opposition from all departments of the administration as well as the press because of the inevitable increased costs to the consumer and taxpayer.

Innovation, improved fleet management, and productivity enhancement as well as renewed reliance on free market forces to alleviate the problems plaguing the American shipping industry were virtually ignored in the Commission report. In a 23 February 1989 editorial commenting on the Commission's work, the *Journal of Commerce* observed:

> Its final report, released last week, is less a compendium of promising ideas than a stirring call to a return to the 1940s. . . . By failing to address the commercial viability of U.S. shipping and offering no politically feasible program, the Commission on Merchant Marine and Defense has ensured that its report, like many that have come before it, will gather dust.

While going overboard in its attempt to support the shipbuilders, the Commission did conclude that an inadequate shipbuilding base for commercial ships *only* affects the long-term mobilization posture in the event of a protracted, nonnuclear war. This scenario was chosen to justify the proposed $13 billion program. While from the standpoint of the defense planners this possibility cannot be ruled out, given the existing severe mobilization and production problems in all of America industry, the U.S. shipbuilding base looks relatively good by comparison.

It seems obvious that for any real progress to be made, the shipbuilding industry must stand on its own two feet and no longer be allowed to dictate merchant marine policy. An industry that received $50.2 billion in government appropriations between 1984 and 1986 and for which more than $60 billion in appropriations have been and are proposed for fiscal years 1987 through 1991 cannot claim lack of federal support.

What the Commission mistakenly identified as an industry problem actually applies only to a small group of companies that cannot compete in the construction of U.S. naval vessels. With the inauguration of the program to build a "600-ship Navy," the nation's shipbuilders have turned almost exclusively to naval ship construction. In the process of doing this, they undoubtedly have become the finest in the world. However, the ability to successfully obtain government contracts and build to Navy specifications requires skills only remotely related to commercial ship construction. The talents required to market, finance, and compete for commercial contracts are quite different from those required to profitably obtain government business.

The impression that "the shipbuilding industry is going out of business unless domestic commercial ship building is restored" is inaccurate and seems to confuse and mislead the Congress. Because it goes unchallenged, it has been generally accepted. To draw the unsubstantiated conclusion that the possible decline of this small sector of the current shipbuilding industry imperils national security defies logic.

With the new administration struggling with massive budget deficits and at the same time seeking new funding to finance the president's war on drugs, the Commission's $13 billion program appears to many to be completely unrealistic. Not daunted, on 23 May, Maritime Day, Chairman Bennett and Walter Jones (D-NC), chairman of the House Merchant Marine and Fisheries Committee, announced their co-sponsorship of HR 2463, a bill intended to provide the enabling legislation to bring the Commission's recommendation into being.

An event that had happened a few months earlier, however, cast a somber shadow over the Maritime Day proceedings. In the early hours of 24 March, the *Exxon Valdez*, a modern 213,000 DWT tanker, fully laden with Alaskan crude oil, ran aground in Prince William Sound, ripping a large hole in its bottom and rupturing several of its cargo tanks. The widespread oil pollution and resulting damage to wildlife and the ecology was devastating. The cause of the accident, according to initial reports, seemed to have resulted from the ship's having deviated from its designated course. This was attributed to a piloting error on the part of the ship's captain, possibly compounded by

■ *Outward bound after loading U.S. military cargo destined for an international training exercise overseas is one of the Military Sealift Command's eight fast sealift ships.*

a lack of appropriate, timely action on the part of the watch officer.

The investigation of the accident will be a long one. It is certain to generate numerous legislative proposals, dealing more with the effect of the oil spill than its possible cause. One of the immediate charges by a maritime union official was that the accident somehow was related to the company's recent reduction in shipboard manning scales. The official claimed that with more men on the ship, the grounding could somehow have been prevented. The state of Alaska is currently seeking billions of dollars in damages, contending that the company was negligent not only in the construction of the vessel but, picking up on the union official's allegation, also charging that the ship was undermanned.

Raising the question of manning scales at this time is unfortunate. The U.S. Coast Guard has been reviewing the laws and regulations relating to required manning scales and working conditions on U.S. vessels for some time. Such claims relating to the *Exxon Valdez* have a tendency to politicize the issue when it should be judged on merit alone. Most of the U.S. laws relating to the employment of seamen were enacted early in this century and need revision. While a number of the maritime labor unions understand and accept the need for modernization, there are others that are actively opposed to any such move. Should this latter group be successful, the result will be to place the American shipowner farther behind his foreign competition and increasingly dependent on subsidies.

To date, U.S. legal and regulatory agencies have been of little help in this effort to modernize ship-board operations. Generally they can be described as grudgingly accepting advances made in other countries rather than actively encouraging U.S. owners to be on the leading edge of these advances. The immediate changes that are required are (1) The elimination of the three-man watch system; (2) Removal of all impediments to cross-utilization of shipboard personnel, that is, the interchange of personnel between the deck and engine rooms; and (3) The elimination of the requirement for a dedicated radio officer on off-shore vessels.

Absent any administration effort to really push for legislation to remove these noncompetitive working conditions and manning requirements, the shipowners continue to depend on subsidies as the primary solution to the problems arising from their higher costs. In August 1989 the United Ship Owners of America (USA), an association representing the subsidized and unsubsidized U.S. liner companies, unveiled its proposal to reform the subsidy program. Like its previous recommendations, a new law it proposes would:

1. Allow the purchase of foreign-built ships;
2. Provide operating differential subsidy (ODS) to all qualified operators; and
3. Deregulate the international trade route system.

While these provisions are not new, there is a change, since for the first time all of the members of USA are in agreement on this approach.

The proposal for "reform" is somewhat misleading, since it is intended to extend ODS eligibility without requiring any reduction in the existing wage-cost structure.

To demonstrate the need for subsidy extension, the president of USA has given the following example:

> A U.S. Flag liner company with 20 modern automated diesel vessels with 21-man crews starts off at a disadvantage each year of $40 to $50 million for its fleet. Thus, if an American operator is exactly as competitive and efficient as his foreign competitor with 20 similar ships, he will lose $40 to $50 million per year while the foreigner breaks even.

This example, while accurate for the subsidized operators, generally misstates the cost-differential for most of those who receive no subsidy. For these latter companies, the differential is substantially less than that indicated. Also, the extent of this wage-cost disparity applies only when the comparison is made with low-cost Filipino and Asian crews. If the cost differential analysis is made with South American crews, for example, it would be considerably less.

For most nonsubsidized companies, the crew costs today are essentially competitive with those countries enjoying a similar standard of living, such as Germany, the Scandinavian countries, and even Japan. However, most of these countries are rapidly lowering their crew size to 14 men or even less. Under existing law the American owner cannot take similar action. For the administration to support any extension of ODS, it is believed that some element of "reform" in the form of built-in incentives for crew-cost reductions will have to be incorporated in the package.

The effort to lower crew costs and to more fully use the available technology has surfaced as another significant problem for the shipowner in 1989. That is the requirement to raise substantially the level of crew training. The smaller crews have to be more highly trained than those previously, when the necessary skills now required for one man were dispersed over several people. Most of the foreign companies that have utilized reduced manning scales have undertaken significant training programs to enable them to properly and safely bring about the necessary changes. At least one American company and one of the maritime labor unions are beginning similar programs.

Even with their 14-man crews, the Germans and Scandinavians are still at a significant cost disadvantage versus the Asian crews. One means of preserving some of the national benefits of the home flag in the face of this ever-increasing cost pressure is currently being developed in Europe. That is, the establishment of international ship registries. Most of these countries, lacking any national-defense requirements, are unwilling to subsidize crew wages, although there is some consideration of wage-related tax relief. As a consequence, European shipowners, for competitive reasons, have been forced to transfer their ships to third flags. With the establishment of international registries in their own countries, their ships can fly the national flag while being exempted from most of the premium costs associated with national-flag requirements. These registries are in most respects similar to those of Panama or Liberia. Great Britain, Norway, Denmark, Germany, and France all have established these registries in the past year, and others are planning to follow. By mid-1989, the Norwegian International Register (NIS) had some 500 ships listed. Plans to provide for a similar ship registry under the European Community umbrella already are underway.

In July, the Japanese Transport Ministry issued its first public endorsement of legislation that would allow non-Japanese seamen on merchant ships registered in Japan. The All-Japanese Seaman's Union softened its former insistence for all Japanese crews, settling instead for a minimum number of its own nationals in the crew.

What does all of this mean for the United States and the American shipowner? Hopefully, very little. Given the need to maintain a nucleus of highly trained U.S. seamen to man both the Ready Reserve Force (RRF) and the National Defense Reserve Fleet (NDRF) in time of emergency, it is hard to believe that this would present an attractive alternative for defense planners. However, if the administration lacks the political will to provide shipowners the freedom to effectively compete by removal of present restrictions, it is only a question of time before some U.S. shipowners will be driven to a similar course of action.

American shipowners who already own foreign flag tonnage, registered under an assortment of third flags, are facing another aspect of a government created problem. The 1986 tax reform legislation terminated their right to defer earnings that could be invested in shipping assets. This provision is Subpart F of the Internal Revenue Code, and its repeal makes future ownership increasingly unattractive. This revision, adopted in the House without benefit of hearings and later incorporated in the final tax bill, cannot be of help to those elements of maritime labor that lobbied for the change since it hardly will force the owners to undertake the even greater cost of U.S. Flag ownership. It will, however, ultimately further reduce the declining shipping resources that American owners still control. In the Commission's final hearing, Thomas S. Wyman of the Chevron Shipping Company testified:

> . . . under the provisions of the Tax Reform Act of 1986, a U.S. operator of a militarily useful tanker of 80,000 deadweight tons incurs a cost disadvantage of approximately $700,000 per year in the Aruba-New York trade compared to his foreign competitor in the same trade who can defer his tax liabilities.

The underpinning of the tax law as it affects U.S. shipping is the naive assumption that the sealift capabilities conferred by an active merchant marine can be achieved without treating the industry in any way differently from other U.S. industries. Let no one underestimate the importance of this misconception. Today, the competition in the international shipping markets is fierce. No vessel owner will survive for long if he is forced by his government to absorb higher cost differentials, and it is an absolute certainty that the industry will be incapable of attracting the required new capital if obstacles like the new tax laws are left in place.

So, while the Europeans and Japanese are encouraging shipowners to return to national flag registries and in many cases at least gaining employment for key ratings, the American government has succeeded in discouraging continued ownership and the degree of control of these vessels that it formerly exercised. At the request of Congressman Bennett, who seems to understand the consequences of this legislative change, the Government Accounting Office has begun to collect evidence to assess the likely effect of the new tax law upon the Flag of Convenience (FOC) owners in the United States.

One of the few high spots in this otherwise lackluster year was the emergence of a new champion appearing out of the west (if St. Louis can be so classified) in the person of the Commander in Chief, U.S. Transportation Command, Gen. Duane H. Cassidy, USAF, and his very able deputy, Vice Adm. Albert

J. Herberger, USN. These two relative newcomers to the maritime community have demonstrated a clarity of thought on the subject of sealift that has been generally lacking in government circles. Adm. William J. Crowe, Jr. recently retired chairman of the Joint Chiefs of Staff, observed:

> While there is no dearth of sound ideas in this country and in Washington, there is definitely a scarcity of leaders who can recognize a truly worthwhile proposal, flesh it out, drive it through our complex bureaucracy, overcome its nay-sayers, and ultimately develop sufficient public and Congressional support to make it a reality.

Cassidy is such a leader, and he quickly recognized the strategic vulnerability of the nation arising from a rapidly declining U.S. merchant fleet. Lacking essential sealift, it became obvious to him that the country would no longer be able to sustain any major overseas operation in time of war.

At every opportunity, he attempted to alert the administration and the Congress to the full dimension of the problem. At his urging, the National Security Council finally has focused on a statement of National Sealift Policy that emphasizes the necessity for unilateral response capability of the U.S. merchant fleet. While it remains the government's policy to rely on both U.S. and allied shipping resources to meet strategic obligations, the NSC recognized that the country must have an American fleet capable of handling security threats in geographic areas not covered by alliance commitments.

In his last testimony before the Senate Subcommittee on Merchant Marine prior to his September retirement, Cassidy spelled out what he considered to be the essential ingredients of any program to revitalize the U.S. merchant marine. The elements of such a program are:

1. Bring about a complete decoupling of the ship operating and shipbuilding industries.
2. Eliminate government regulations that limit competition. Specifically, repeal the 50 percent ad valorum tax on foreign repairs, and remove all restrictions on the ability of the U.S. shipowners to trade anywhere in the world.
3. Provide a level playing field for shipowners engaged in international competition with regard to their obligations under the U.S. Tax Code, i.e., restore rights enjoyed prior to the 1986 Tax Reform Legislation.
4. Provide ODS to all qualified ships. Recognize that payment of wage differentials is essential if a nucleus of trained U.S. seamen is to be available to man the RRF and NDRF.
5. Take the necessary steps to ensure that the U.S. merchant marine carries a fair share of our international trade. This share should be commensurate with those carried by the ships of our trading partners.

What Cassidy was trying to impress on the President and the Congress was that this country once again could become a major participant in the international shipping community if they both would fo-

■ *Finding it increasingly more difficult to compete with foreign shipping lines are U.S. firms such as American President Lines, whose container ship President Eisenhower is underway with a full load of containers.*

cus effectively on the sealift problem and then exercise the political courage to remove the government-imposed restrictions that stifle future growth. Regrettably, though, the fact that the U.S. merchant fleet could be revitalized without any substantial increase in the present level of funding appears to be of little interest. And while all sides preach austerity, Congress had no difficulty in appropriating $600 million in FY 1990–1991 for the design and construction of fast sealift ships.

Another encouraging sign was the confirmation in October of Warren Leback as the new Maritime Administrator. Few in the shipping community could bring the wealth of industry and government experience to that position that Leback does. He is no stranger to the job, as he successfully served for several years as the deputy administrator. The industry, the Congress, and the nation will be looking to him to clearly and forcefully articulate and implement the Bush Administration's future maritime policies.

As required by the Shipping Act of 1984 (the Act), the Federal Maritime Commission (FMC) undertook a review of the effect of the Act after five years of operation. This law undoubtedly was the single most important piece of maritime legislation enacted in the 1980s. It streamlined the FMC's rate-agreement procedures, redefined antitrust immunity for carriers, and permitted rationalization of services. The FMC's study, issued in September, makes no firm recommendations for change and is primarily a compendium of the testimony given by the interested parties during its hearings. The Act will undoubtedly be subject of further review.

In mid-summer, the FMC also began a far-ranging investigation of the unfair trading practices that two American carriers, APL and SeaLand, have faced in Taiwan. This is the first use of the new powers contained in the 1988 Trade Act to conduct such an investigation. These provisions were specifically designed to combat actions either promoted or permitted by foreign governments that are prejudicial to American shipping interests. An adverse finding by the FMC could subject a nation's merchant marine to severe sanctions involving trade with the United States.

It is anticipated that this is only the first of a number of such actions, and its outcome will be carefully assessed to determine the extent of the U.S. government's resolve to fight discrimination. After years of largely fruitless attempts to encourage the State Department to take similar action, the provisions of the 1988 Act, if vigorously enforced by the FMC, could bring a new era of trading opportunities for the American shipping industry.

In another action claiming foreign discrimination, the Shipbuilders Council of America (SCA) filed a petition under Section 301 of the amended 1974 Trade Act with the U.S. Trade Representative (USTR). The petition charged Norway, Germany, Japan, and South Korea with unfairly providing shipbuilding subsidies. The USTR, Carla Hill, indicated that she will pursue the complaint through two multinational agencies—the Organization of Economic Cooperation and Development (OECD) and the General Agreement on Tariffs and Trade (GATT). She further stated that if these talks do not bring significant results, she would undertake a formal investigation in March 1990.

The president of the SCA stated that ". . . the goal of the petition was to get the U.S. government to recognize the role foreign subsidies have played in the devastation of U.S. commercial ship construction. . . ." Looked at on its merits, this is a rather unusual assertion since the U.S. yards have never indicated the slightest interest in participating in the international shipbuilding market. Indeed, for decades their main effort has been directed solely to maintaining a captive market in the United States. One objective of the petition may be to divert attention from the extremely low level of shipbuilding productivity in the United States.

During the course of the hearings conducted by the Commission, it received expert testimony that shipbuilding productivity in the best U.S. yards was approximately half of that of the average German and Japanese yards. Leonard Course, manager of maintenance and repair for the Chevron Shipping Company, demonstrated that the cost of new ship construction in the United States ranged from two to three times that for a similar ship in the Far East. Since shipyard labor rates are roughly equal in the United States and Japan, he concluded that the difference in shipbuilding costs appeared to be attributable to ". . . a combination of antiquated technology, poor management practices, and low labor productivity."

The foregoing judgment may be overly harsh, since the major U.S. shipbuilders have continued to invest substantially in improving and upgrading their construction technology. During FY 1988 they are reported to have invested $145 million, and in FY 1989 had formulated plans to invest more than $65 million, to improve their competitiveness and efficiency for future participation in the Navy's construction, repair, and overhaul projects. In its 1988 annual report released early in 1989, the Maritime Administration noted that the nation's shipbuilders had invested some $4.2 billion in facility improvements during the past 20 years.

The Commission's recommended "build and charter" program best illustrates the only market in which the U.S. yards seem to have any real interest. As proposed, the government would be obligated to design, finance, and finally purchase the ships being built. It also would undoubtedly have to absorb the consequences of production delays and cost overruns. Such a proposal bears no resemblance to commercial shipbuilding practices.

In 1989, after many years of reduced demand and depressed prices, the level of world shipyard prices began to rise significantly. In addition to increased demand for new buildings, the reasons for these changes are (1) An appreciation of Japanese and Korean currencies, (2) Substantial wage increases in Korea following the prolonged strikes earlier in the year, and (3) Considerable reduction in world shipyard capacity in the past 10 years. Given the current weakness of the U.S. dollar, and highly competitive U.S. shipyard wage levels, the time would seem ripe to aggressively enter the world shipbuilding marketplace. U.S. shipbuilders undoubtedly have the innate ability to do this. If the government wants to help, it would remove the laws that are intended to provide them with a captive market. There is ample evidence that this has not worked, and the removal of this vain hope might encourage them to look to a competitive world instead of a nonexistent, government-restricted market, as their source of new business.

On what may be a final note of irony for the year, the Department of Transportation launched another series of studies to develop a national transportation policy. The DOT Director of International Transportation and Trade said in an interview that part of the study was intended to examine ". . . the maritime policy question from which all others flow," and that is "how to make the merchant marine competitive to the point it can fill its national security requirements." This is certainly a most fair question, and his answer will be awaited with interest. The study is due to be completed early in 1990.

One can only hope that this latest initiative for DOT will at least get the numbers straight. First, it should recognize that there is absolutely no cost to the U.S. taxpayer in acquiring a modern competitive fleet, if it is obtained and maintained in the world market. Second, it should be fully aware that the wage-cost differential for American seamen currently paid in the form of ODS does not reflect the prevailing cost for most of the nonsubsidized operators or the crews directly employed by the Military Sealift Command (MSC). With the elimination of the barriers to reaching optimum manning scales, the wage differential would be further reduced. The remaining difference in cost can properly be rationalized as a naval reserve payment associated with the RRF and NDRF and if paid directly to the seamen would remove the "subsidy" stigma once and for all.

The vast changes that have been going on in the Kremlin and in Eastern Europe during the year may, in the long run, prove to have the greater effect on the American merchant marine and its role in the national defense than any of the proposed changes. Because of the lessening world tensions, the warning factor, i.e., the time available to prepare for the outbreak of hostilities, is certain to be extended. The requirement for fast response sealift, now maintained at significant cost, may well be reduced.

Another aspect of this change will inevitably be the reduction of U.S. forces stationed overseas. This process already is beginning. One should not have to be reminded that any of the Russian forces eventually withdrawn can be rapidly reintroduced over well-developed rail and highway systems. The United States, on the other hand, has no such ready access. The only avenue available is over the 3,000 miles of the Atlantic Ocean. Logic would seem to dictate that this would result in an even greater need for sealift augmentation if we are to maintain a forward strategy in support of our allies. In the past, however, such rational thinking rarely has prevailed.

One of the well-documented characteristics of the American people as reflected in our political system is generally to react to a crisis only after it has happened. Throughout our 200-year history, when the crisis was over, there invariably has been a determined effort to restrict our naval and maritime resources. This is inevitable for a program that relies primarily on war or the single-minded efforts of a president to sustain it.

It is only on rare occasions that our government has recognized that a merchant marine is of sufficient importance to develop well-conceived and well-coordinated programs and then to implement them fully. These occasions have been either in time of war or when we have had a president who could comprehend the relationship of sea power and America's interests.

In the last century, three presidents have demonstrated this understanding. Theodore Roosevelt connected the two great oceans with the Panama Canal, resulting in a major increase in American trade. At the same time he built a modern American Navy—the "Great White Fleet"—as a demonstration of American political and economic interests as an emerging world power.

Franklin Roosevelt used the rebuilding of the Navy in the 1930s as an economic tool, followed by rebuilding the U.S. merchant marine. His efforts—naval and merchant—were key factors in our overwhelming victory in World War II.

Support for rebuilding the U.S. merchant marine was once again forthcoming in 1969, when the most recent maritime program was developed. Richard Nixon clearly understood the nation's need to promote and maintain its maritime strength and the result was the Merchant Marine Act of 1970.

As we enter the last decade of the 20th century, the responsibility for developing a new program rests squarely with President Bush. To succeed, such a program must be carefully crafted, skillfully oriented politically, and presidentially directed. Without this last, the best that can be hoped for is minimal progress based on both endless compromise and unnecessary expense. But no president can be expected to take on such a task unless he is personally persuaded that there is a real and urgent national need to do so.

GTE Communication Systems

- **Tactical data link systems.** Multifrequency data link systems and components – modems, multirate voice terminals, neural network controllers and network management systems – for data and voice applications.

- **Tactical C² systems.** Communication systems and networks in support of Navy tactical command and control applications.

For a free copy of a calendar featuring this photo, call the Marketing Manager, Navy Systems, at 617-455-3728, fax him at 617-455-5888, or write to the address shown at the right.

✱ *The AN/PRC-114(V) low-power, secure transceiver and flight-deck-certified, noise-occluding helmet are parts of the*